Joomla! Accessibility

A quick guide to creating accessible websites with Joomla!

Joshue O Connor

PUBLISHING

BIRMINGHAM - MUMBAI

Joomla! Accessibility

First published: October 2007

Production Reference: 1231007

Published by Packt Publishing Ltd.
32 Lincoln Road
Olton
Birmingham, B27 6PA, UK.

ISBN 978-1-847194-08-4

www.packtpub.com

Cover Image by Vinayak Chittar (vinayak.chittar@gmail.com)

Credits

Author

  Joshue O Connor

Reviewers

  Niko Kotiniemi

  Joseph LeBlanc

Senior Acquisition Editor

  David Barnes

Development Editor

  Mithil Kulkarni

Technical Editor

  Akshara Aware

Editorial Manager

  Dipali Chittar

Project Manager

  Abhijeet Deobhakta

Project Coordinator

  Abhijeet Deobhakta

Indexer

  Monica Ajmera

Proofreader

  Damian Carvill

Production Coordinator

  Aparna Bhagat

Cover Designer

  Aparna Bhagat

About the Author

Joshue O Connor is a Senior Accessibility Consultant with CFIT (Centre For Inclusive Technology).

CFIT is a part of the NCBI (National Council For The Blind of Ireland) and is a non-profit organisation that provides expert advice and services to public and private sector organizations. These services include user testing, accessibility auditing, and consultancy.

Joshue has a creative background in Graphic Design, which lead to Web Development and New Media Training. After several years in the shark infested waters of the private sector, through IT training, he got to work with people with a wide range of physical and cognitive disabilities.

This was an invaluable hands-on experience that brought him into contact with a diverse range of assistive technology users, who found technology a positive and enabling force in their lives. A natural gravitation towards web accessibility thus blossomed.

Joshue is skilled in the design and development of accessible websites and has a deep understanding of the diversity of user requirements. He is a member of the Guild of Accessible Web Designers (GAWDS), the Web Standards Project ILG (WaSP ILG), the Irish Design For All E-Accessibility Network (Irl-Dean), the IIA User Experience Working Group (UEWG), EUAIN, and the HTML 5 Working group.

This is his first book, contributions to obscure academic papers notwithstanding.

In his spare time he hangs out with his plants, studies computer science, plays traditional Irish music badly, and runs a small record label at www.techrecord.net.

I would like to dedicate the book to my father Michael J O Connor.

I would like to thank:

Jared Smith (WebAIM), Gez Lemon (Juicy Studio), Mike Cherim (Green Beast), Mark Magennis (CFIT), Paul Traynor (NCBI), Stuart Lawler (NCBI), Laura Carlson (University of Minnesota Duluth), Vlad Alexander (XStandard), Steve Faulkner (WAT-C), Patrick H. Lauke (Splintered.co.uk).

About the Reviewers

Niko Kotiniemi has a background the service sector, Union and Unemployment Fund related work as well as the travel sector. In 2004 he turned his lifelong computer hobby to into a living, starting with custom web projects and open-source CMS systems. Since the very beginning of his computer related career he has worked with Mambo and later with Joomla!. In 2006, at the age of 30 he decided to obtain the academic qualifications and entered Software Engineering studies at the Helsinki Polytechnic Stadia, Information Technology department.

During the course of his studies he is constantly working on different web-projects to both finance his studies as well as out of professional interest. Most of his free time is spent with family and in studying new trends and technologies and ways in which they can be integrated to real-life situations such as those faced by private entrepreneurs and small companies. Currently his main technological interests lie in Joomla!, wiki's, all of the Google labs products, Ajax, Gadgets/Widgets, databases and specialized websites for niche groups.

You can reach him through his personal website `http://www.kotiniemi.fi` or through e-mail: niko@kotiniemi.fi

Joseph L. LeBlanc started with computers at a very young age. His independent education gave him the flexibility to experiment and learn computer science. Joseph holds a bachelor's degree in Management Information Systems from Oral Roberts University.

Joseph is currently a freelance Joomla! extension developer. He released a popular component tutorial in May 2004, then later authored the book, Learning Joomla! 1.5 Extension Development: Creating Modules, Components, and Plugins with PHP. Work samples and open-source extensions are available at `www.jlleblanc.com`. In addition to freelancing, he is a board member of the DC PHP Conference. He has also worked as a programmer for a web communications firm in Washington, DC.

Table of Contents

Preface

Joomla! is one of the best open-source Content Management Systems available. Joomla! can be used to create accessible feature rich websites, Joomla! also has one of the most accessible back-end interfaces. This means that Joomla! can be used as a development tool by users of Assistive Technology (AT).

If you have no experience of interacting with people with disabilities then it can be very difficult to successfully design user interfaces that cover their needs. The book aims to help you understand and appreciate these needs and guides you through some of the technologies used to interact with computers and the web.

The book looks at why accessibility should be on your radar, from accessibility as a component of best practice, to legislative or legal requirements. The book aims to help you understand accessibility and create websites that can be used by everyone, and how Joomla! can help you to achieve this.

What This Book Covers

Chapter 1 looks at the legal situation around the world and other drivers that put accessibility on the web developer's map. This chapter also looks at some definitions of accessibility and introduces the concepts of usability and universality. The chapter explores the need to understand your users, accommodate diversity and dealing with change as well as some of the benefits of accessibility.

Chapter 2 considers how both accessibility and usability make up a powerful combination for a holistic approach to web development and a positive user experience for everyone. The chapter looks at other practical ways of determining whether your sites are not only accessible but also usable, such as user testing. The chapter also looks at the Web Content Accessibility Guidelines (WCAG).

Chapter 3 looks at various types of disability as well as the variety of assistive technology that is available. You will also learn how to modify your browsing experience in order to try and gain a greater understanding of what it is like for people with disabilities when they go online.

Chapter 4 looks at using headings and other HTML elements to provide content structure. How this benefits users of assistive technology and other SEO (Search Engine Optimization) benefits. This chapter examines how to provide simple text alternatives to images and using descriptive link text to assist accessibility, as well as creating accessible tables and how to edit the HTML by hand.

Chapter 5 examines the importance of preparation while designing your template and the advantages of using accessible templates. The chapter also explains the importance of good color contrast and making your text resizable for visually impaired users as well as the making your interface keyboard accessible.

Chapter 6 looks at getting the most out of XStandard. Throughout most of the book, TinyMCE is used.

Who is This Book for

This book is a guide to any Joomla! user who wants to make their sites more accessible. It does assume basic knowledge of working with Joomla!. You don't need to know anything about accessibility—the author tells you all that you need to know to make your Joomla! sites compliant with accessibility standards.

While some design skills and technical knowledge of HTML, CSS and PHP will be very useful you will still benefit from reading this book if you wish to understand more about assistive technology and the needs of people with disabilities. The book is distilled from years of hands on experience that the author has as a web developer and also working with people with disabilities.

Conventions

In this book, you will find a number of styles of text that distinguish between different kinds of information. Here are some examples of these styles, and an explanation of their meaning.

There are three styles for code. Code words in text are shown as follows: "We can include other contexts through the use of the `include` directive."

A block of code will be set as follows:

```xml
<?xml version="1.0" encoding="iso-8859-1"?>
<install version="1.5" type="template">
  <name>Music</name>
  <version>1.0.0</version>
```

New terms and **important words** are introduced in a bold-type font. Words that you see on the screen, in menus or dialog boxes for example, appear in our text like this: "clicking the **Next** button moves you to the next screen".

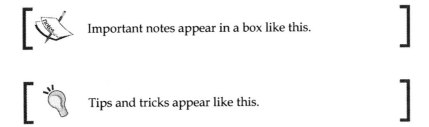

Important notes appear in a box like this.

Tips and tricks appear like this.

Reader Feedback

Feedback from our readers is always welcome. Let us know what you think about this book, what you liked or may have disliked. Reader feedback is important for us to develop titles that you really get the most out of.

To send us general feedback, simply drop an email to `feedback@packtpub.com`, making sure to mention the book title in the subject of your message.

If there is a book that you need and would like to see us publish, please send us a note in the **SUGGEST A TITLE** form on `www.packtpub.com` or email `suggest@packtpub.com`.

If there is a topic that you have expertise in and you are interested in either writing or contributing to a book, see our author guide on `www.packtpub.com/authors`.

Customer Support

Now that you are the proud owner of a Packt book, we have a number of things to help you to get the most from your purchase.

Errata

Although we have taken every care to ensure the accuracy of our contents, mistakes do happen. If you find a mistake in one of our books—maybe a mistake in text or code—we would be grateful if you would report this to us. By doing this you can save other readers from frustration, and help to improve subsequent versions of this book. If you find any errata, report them by visiting http://www.packtpub. com/support, selecting your book, clicking on the **Submit Errata** link, and entering the details of your errata. Once your errata are verified, your submission will be accepted and the errata added to the list of existing errata. The existing errata can be viewed by selecting your title from http://www.packtpub.com/support.

Questions

You can contact us at questions@packtpub.com if you are having a problem with some aspect of the book, and we will do our best to address it.

1
Why be Accessible?

To get started, we will first look at what accessibility is. We will look at the benefits of accessibility, as well as some of the drivers behind the scenes, such as legislations around the world.

You may already have an appreciation (and I hope that you do) that making your websites and interfaces accessible is the right thing to do. No one wants to be discriminatory, block users out of their sites, or frustrate them with bad design and poor code. Most websites that are guilty of this are probably not even aware of it. However, even though many of the websites around the world are still inaccessible – this is slowly changing. I hope that this introduction, and the following chapters, will help you become a little more informed of what it is that we are trying to do here and why.

Defining Accessibility

There are several definitions of accessibility. The International Standards Organization (ISO) defines accessibility as:

> *"The usability of a product, service, environment or facility by people with the widest range of capabilities (ISO TC 16071)."*

If we apply this definition to the Web it refers to the design interfaces and applications that can be used by the widest possible audience; ensuring that there are no users who are left out when trying to use them. That's great, however, note that it doesn't specifically mention blind users or other people with disabilities at all, yet it talks about **usability**.

The W3C in its "Introduction to Web Accessibility", defines it as:

"Web accessibility means that people with disabilities can use the Web. More specifically, Web accessibility means that people with disabilities can perceive, understand, navigate, and interact with the Web, and that they can contribute to the Web. Web accessibility also benefits others, including older people with changing abilities due to aging."

You can read further at: `http://www.w3.org/WAI/intro/accessibility.php`

So some definitions specifically talk about people with disabilities and others don't. While I believe that access for everyone is a great ideal, I also think that the details are important, and I support the definition that specifically mentions people with disabilities. According to me the first definition, talks about **universality**, which is great, but I think that web accessibility is a specific part of that universal umbrella that mostly relates to people with disabilities. As you read further you will realize that people with disabilities have specific needs; and in order to meet these needs, you as an author or developer, need some solid techniques and understanding, so that they can use your website easily. This is where I hope this book will be useful.

Understanding Your Users

Whatever definition you prefer, the upshot is that it is important to understand your audience and their different needs. How can you do that? I have been very fortunate as I got some experience as a graphic designer/developer and IT trainer in the private sector before I got to work directly with people with disabilities and assistive technology (AT). So I experienced some really positive effects that simple technologies and good designs can have on people with disabilities.

I am currently working with blind and visually impaired people, but what informs my definition and experience of accessibility, as well as my understanding of the diversity of user requirements, does not stop there. Many people think that web accessibility is mostly about serving the needs of visually impaired users. However, this is not true. The truth is that by serving the needs of the blind and visually impaired users, you will actually improve the accessibility and usability of your website or software for everyone. Again, this can be seen as a happy by-product of good practice and development habits on your part.

Dealing with Change

In many ways accessibility encompasses our ability to deal with change and to cope with diversity. There are changes, such as failing sight and other physical and mental changes that we go through as we get older. Therefore our abilities to perform certain tasks and the equipment we need to do the every day tasks may also change. I may need glasses to read or at least play my music much louder (though that may be why I am going deaf!). Whatever it is we will invariably find that our own abilities change with time.

Understanding accessibility involves stretching our abilities to deal with these changes and user diversity. The success of your efforts, to quite a large degree, depends on how well you can accommodate diverse user requirements in your web projects.

Think Different

Apart from being a well known advertising slogan for some computer manufacturer, the above heading is also a good piece of advice and is helpful in understanding accessibility. Often, there are barriers for users in places that you may never dream of. You will also find that many solutions result from doing things the right way and not cutting corners in your work. The following are some examples, and while they are not all Web related, I hope they will get you thinking about how you could get around some accessibility issues from both the Web and the built environment.

These examples are from the NCBI CFIT website (www.cfit.ie):

1. A bank cash machine presents information and choices using a video screen only, so the blind customers cannot use it.

2. A home alarm system indicates if it is set correctly using sounds only, but an elderly person who finds it difficult to hear cannot tell the sounds apart.

3. A website specifies a small fixed size for text, so a user with low vision cannot use the built-in browser controls to increase it to a size they can read.

4. The input slot on a ticket machine is out of reach for a person sitting in a wheelchair, so they cannot use it.

5. The buttons on a remote control are too close together and fiddly to operate for an older person with arthritis.

6. A web page has too much content and is confusingly laid out, so it takes too long for many people to find the information they want on it.

In short you often have to think outside the box, look at problems from different angles, and analyze the situation, to come up with a workable solution.

What Are the Benefits of Accessibility?

There are some substantial benefits of accessible web design and development:

- **It makes good business sense**: Who would want to limit the amount of their product or service that they can sell? Not many, or if that is the case then they will not be in business for long. Building accessible websites can actually increase the amount of business you do by ensuring that no one is excluded from your website. So effectively you allow anyone who is interested to enter, treat them well, and ensure that their stay is a pleasant one.

- **Enhanced SEO (Search Engine Optimization)**: SEO can seem to be a black art (and for some it literally is). If you are a little unsure of what to do to get your business-website ranking improved don't fear — make your site accessible and it's ranking will certainly improve. This is because search engines (including Google) can be thought of as blind users. If you structure your content well and make it accessible — then search engines will be able to search your content more quickly, find appropriate keywords, and serve your pages with a higher ranking for relevant keyword searches.

Search engines like Google often change their secret algorithm, and many try to anticipate these changes, and hack their HTML accordingly. This is a waste of time.

You will be much better off creating a nice accessible site rather than performing keyword stuffing, abusing alt tags, and other bad, black hat SEO practices.

- **Better design**: Graphic designers unfortunately, often design for themselves. This is not always the case, but is often true. As a result the Web is littered with sites that use tiny text that can't be resized, illegible fonts, and bad color contrast. This often renders the site content unreadable to many — though in the designer's head it looks great.

So by considering the diverse needs of users, for example, people with vision impairment who need good color contrast and resizable text, the designers should change their styles to accommodate these user's needs. A good design principle is that "form should follow function". This is a simple, but effective mantra. Unfortunately, it is often completely ignored.

Accessibility brings some important design issues back into sharp focus and designers must rethink how they are going present content, their layout techniques and so on.

How you design can have both a powerful positive and negative impact, so don't just follow fashion, think about your users.

"Accessibility is not anti-design". Many of your cool graphic designer friends might believe this. They are laboring under a misconception. Accessibility actually forces them to think about the details and motivation behind what they design, forcing them to not vainly follow trends, or use their design skills only to express themselves.

Tell them if they wish to express themselves they should join a punk band, otherwise they should think about what they are doing and ensure that lazy or shallow fashionable design styles do not dictate how they work.

If you have an awkward client who refuses to see reason when it comes to good design, firstly take a deep breath, and try explaining the reasons for your design decisions. This means with careful use of logic and good reasoning you can usually beat any fuzzy ideas your client has about their perception of what constitutes a good design.

Accessibility Legislation

You might have to ensure that your website is accessible under certain laws. This however depends on which part of the world you are in, the site's purpose, and several other factors.

We will now look in detail at the current state of legislation in the Ireland, after that we will look at the EU, US, and UK. You can visit the link from the WAI (Web Accessibility Initiative) site that deals with global legislation, if you do not belong to any of these areas.

Much of the following section on Irish legislation comes from the NCBI CFIT website thanks to its author, my colleague, Mark Magennis.

Irish Legislation

There have been significant positive moves in legislation and public policy relating to IT accessibility in Ireland.

The accessibility of online services is mainly covered by "The Disability Act (2005)" and it contains an explicit requirement for public sector bodies. Section 28 states:

> *"Where a public body communicates in electronic form with one or more persons, the head of the body shall ensure that as far as practicable, the contents of the communication are accessible to persons with a visual impairment to whom adaptive technology is available."*

This is a good step towards meeting the needs of visually impaired people. Though it doesn't explicitly cover the needs of other people with different kinds of disabilities, there have been significant advances made in Ireland recently.

The National Disability Authority (NDA) has also produced a Code of Practice on Accessibility of Public Services, which explains the public sector obligation to provide accessible services. The Code has legal gravitas as it states that public websites should be reviewed to ensure they achieve Double-A conformance rating with WCAG 1.0 (Web Content Accessibility Guidelines. We will discuss WCAG in greater detail later in the book.

Accessible Procurement

The NDA also produced a Public Procurement Toolkit, which can be used to provide advice, guidance, and information for those looking for accessible services.

Several other acts have been passed in Ireland, which when viewed as a legislative suite, reflect some positive change. There is "The Equal Status Act (2000)", which requires all service providers to accommodate the needs of people with disabilities by making reasonable changes in what they do and how they do it—without these changes, it would be very difficult or impossible for people with disabilities to obtain these goods or services.

Although not specifically mentioned, this could in theory cover ICT-based services. This follows from the application of similar general disability legislation in Australia and the USA.

However, the Act requires only accommodations that cost a nominal amount. This rules out any but the most trivial efforts. There has never been a test case of this requirement.

The "Employment Equality Act (1998)" covers the provision of accessible technologies to employees. However, like the Equal Status Act, only accommodations that cost a nominal amount are required. There has never been a test case of this requirement.

Laws and Public Policies in Other Countries

Many countries have a legislation that can be applied to all kinds of ICT accessibility including the Web. This usually comes in one of two forms:

- Specific legislation covering public sector services delivered through ICT.
- General disability legislation covering equality of treatment, but not specific to ICT.

The first form (e.g. the U.S. Section 508) usually states specifically that the services delivered through ICT systems must be accessible to people with disabilities. However, this type of legislation usually applies only to the public bodies.

The second form (e.g. the UK Disability Discrimination Act) does not usually mention ICT systems, so it is up to the courts to decide on a case-by-case basis whether it covers things like websites. However, it usually applies to private organizations as well as public bodies.

UK Legislation

Much effective UK legislation is covered by the following three acts:

- Disability Discrimination Act 1995 (DDA)
- Disability Rights Commission Act 1999
- Special Educational Needs and Disability Act 2001, which amended the DDA to provide an obligation in an educational context ('the SENDA').

While the UK guidelines tend to not mention IT explicitly, the code of practice implies the importance of accessible websites. For example, in section 5 of 'Auxiliary Aids and Services' there is as an example of a service and its website that is subject to the DDA.

> *"An airline company provides a flight reservation and booking service to the public on its website. This is a provision of a service and is subject to the Act."*

The DDA was introduced to end the discrimination of people with disabilities by providing access to goods and services, employment rights, and rights when buying or renting property. The "Special Educational Needs and Disability Act of 2001" was passed, which meant that universities had to ensure that their educational services were accessible to disabled learners, as a condition of their grant, as this was not covered in the original DDA (1995).

The US and Section 508/504

The US has taken a rights-based approach. They have also designed their system so that if you do business (or hope to do business) with the federal government, your website and other ancillary services must be accessible. It is a fantastic approach that got the attention of the business community, and has already done a huge amount to raise awareness about accessibility.

Thanks to Jared Smith of WebAIM, where I got much of the following.

The "Rehabilitation Act", which was passed in 1973, secured equal rights for people with disabilities. It was amended to include two sections 504 and 508 that relate to web accessibility.

Section 504 is a civil rights law. It states:

> *"No otherwise qualified individual with a disability in the United States... shall, solely by reason of her or his disability, be excluded from participation in, be denied the benefits of, or be subjected to discrimination under any program or activity receiving Federal financial assistance."*

The language of this legislation is straightforward and unambiguous, and anyone who receives funds from the government may not discriminate against people with disabilities—for example, by having inaccessible web services. This includes schools, government agencies, and universities.

Section 508—as we know it today—refers to an amendment to the Reauthorized Rehabilitation Act of 1998 and it bars the Federal government from procuring inaccessible electronic and information technology (E&IT) goods and services—this includes the Internet.

There are several bodies set up to help guide the standards. They include the Access Board and the EITAAC (Electronic and Information Technology Access and Advisory Committee).

So What's the Big Deal with 508?

Section 508 may be limited only to the federal government, but it had an enormous effect in the private sector.

Section 508 provided the first-ever US federal accessibility standard for the Internet. The Web Content Accessibility Guidelines existed prior to this; however, these guidelines created by the Web Accessibility Initiative (WAI) were not intended to be written as standards. Also, these guidelines came from a voluntary international body with no regulatory power.

This section provides compliance language that could be monitored at a distance. Section 508 outlines binding enforceable standards, which must be adhered to, in order for the E&IT products to be accessible to persons with disabilities. It introduced a statutory language.

State governments may be held accountable for complying with Section 508. All states receive funding under the Assistive Technology Act of 1998. To gain access to this funding, each state must assure the federal government they will implement all conditions of Section 508 within their state entities (including higher education). Many states have codified Section 508 to be state law (e.g., Arizona, Nebraska, and Wisconsin), which requires state institutions to comply with these requirements.

Businesses must comply with Section 508 when supplying Electronic and Information Technology goods and services to the federal government. The influence of web accessibility on business and industry is more significant when the demands of a client, or potential client, like the US federal government, must be met.

All the above points comprise a very big deal and a huge positive step towards inclusive design and accessibility being a standard default setting in providing services to the public.

If someone believes that they have encountered a breach of Section 508 or that they are being discriminated against they may file a private lawsuit in federal district court, or a formal complaint through the US Department of Education Office of Civil Rights.

Section 508 of the Rehabilitation Act has technical standards for all of the following:

- Software Applications and Operating Systems
- Web-based Intranet and Internet Information and Systems
- Telecommunication products
- Video and Multimedia products
- Self contained, closed products
- Desktop and portable computers

The European Union (EU) and e-Accessibility

Different countries within the EU have their own policies to service people with disabilities, rights, etc. We saw the Irish and UK legislation, followed by the situation in the US, and now we will look at the EU policy.

There are several charters, initiatives, and action plans that are in place that make up where the EU is with regard to people with disabilities and accessibility.

The EU Charter of Fundamental Rights has several articles that refer to people with disabilities:

- Article 21 prohibits discrimination based on grounds of disability, among others.
- Article 26 provides explicit recognition of the rights of people with disabilities and the need to ensure their independence, social and occupational integration, and participation in the life of the community.

eEurope Action Plan

The eEurope 2002 and 2005 Action Plans aimed to promote Internet usage and broadband penetration throughout the EU. It looks at how our lives can be benefited by the Internet and accessibility for older people and people with disabilities. You can read further at: http://ec.europa.eu/information_society/eeurope/2005/ index_en.htm

e-Inclusion Policy

The Lisbon Council in 2000 agreed to make a decisive impact to eradicate poverty and social exclusion by 2010. The Riga Ministerial Declaration on e-Inclusion of June 2006 identified six areas that the European Commission views as covering e-Inclusion of which accessibility is a part.

- e-Accessibility: Make ICT accessible for all

- e-Aging: Empower older people and enhance their quality of life.

- e-Competences: Equip citizens with the knowledge, skills, and lifelong learning approach needed to increase social inclusion, employability. and enrich their lives.

- Socio-Cultural e-Inclusion: Enable minorities, migrants and marginalised young people to fully integrate into communities and participate in society by using ICT.

- Geographical e-Inclusion: Increase the social and economic well being of people in rural, remote and economically disadvantaged areas with the help of ICT.

- Inclusive e-Government: Deliver better, more diverse public services for all using ICT while encouraging increased public participation in democracy.

European Policy and the Future

The EU i2010 program is the next step in furthering the goals of e-Inclusion.

The EU has taken a different approach to the US using 'soft legislation' to standardize accessibility requirements for all public procurement, which is hoped to have an effect in the wider market.

The main areas of concern are:

- Accessibility requirements in public procurement
- Certification and assessment
- Exploration of legal measures

So What Does It All Mean to You?

You may be wondering why I have included these rather detailed examples of legislations, standards and policies.

I wish to illustrate that, depending on where in the world you are, how tricky it can be to find clear-cut, unambiguous legislation that clearly states your responsibility under the law. As far as I am concerned, equal access to information and accessible technologies should be a right for everybody and, I really like the US model. However, as I hope that you can now see, in many parts of the world it just isn't so and it is often a struggle to make accessible services a reality in a legislative context.

The US has a rights-based approach where if procurers don't comply, then they don't do business with the federal government, which is one big client to ignore. The EU have adopted a softer 'accessibility as a standard' approach, starting with EU wide procurers (which means public sector agencies) and then taken the view that this will have a trickle down effect for those in the private sector.

Which is the best? It's hard to say. As I mentioned, I like the rights-based approach as I think this got the attention of anyone who wanted to do business with the US government. The EU has taken a different approach.

The US model may engender a 'do the bare minimum' to check all the boxes and declare yourself compliant; this is not an ideal mindset. So only time will tell how effective the EU approach will be. There are many capable people involved in various EU projects who are flying the flag for accessibility and the adoption of best practices and standards.

There is certainly a shift around the world towards public sector and business having to build accessible websites and other ICT services as a matter of course. There have been some high profile court cases, which have brought these accessibility issues into the public consciousness and no doubt there will be more, but even this has not shocked or scared business into a great rush towards making their websites and applications accessible.

Summary

In this chapter we saw some definitions of accessibility and the concepts of usability and universality. We will examine these ideas in greater detail in the next chapter.

We explored the need to understand your users, accommodate diversity, and deal with change. We saw the benefits of accessibility and examined some legislations from around the world.

Although legislation is certainly an effective stick to drive business to create accessible services, some may be of the opinion of paying the fine and ignore users with disabilities, as they are only a small part of the market. If you work for a government department or other public sector agency, bear in mind that your clients are ordinary citizens who have the same right to access information and services as everyone else. The technology to make this a reality already exists!

2
Understanding Accessibility

In this chapter we will examine some other aspects of good user-interface design such as usability. We will look at accessibility as an important component of an holistic approach to web development, as well as what makes good websites and a positive user experience.

We will look at other useful methods for ensuring that your sites are both accessible and usable, such as involving users in the development process through user testing, and if that is not possible, alternatives such as personas are examined.

We will also look at important initiatives to raise the bar in accessible web development such as WCAG (Web Content Accessibility Guidelines).

What Will Joomla! Not Do?

While creating accessible websites with Joomla!, it is also important to understand the limits of the technology.

Joomla! will not magically transform anything the developer or author throws at into structured and accessible content. Although, sometimes we may wish this happens! We often, on a subconscious level, believe that new technology will automatically be able to fix everything so that we could then spend more time hanging out at the beach. However, this is unrealistic. Technological advances have not lead us to lives of leisure, rather we often work harder, deal with more diverse tasks, and for longer hours!

Within the context of using a Content Management System like Joomla! the old adage "garbage in—garbage out" holds true. It is important for you to understand that much of what you can do to create accessible websites comes from what you have acquired over time, with good development and design practices.

The manner in which you approach your web development projects is as important as the tools you use to complete them. More useful work can be done before you even strike a key, by spending time thinking about your project, what you need to achieve and then a sensible way to achieve it. This pre-planning work includes thinking about several diverse threads, information architecture, designing your site's look and feel, and designing simple and intuitive user interfaces.

With my experience I can say that good accessible websites are a by-product of good design. Good design comes from understanding the purpose of your site, understanding your audiences' needs and what they wish to do when using your site.

If you are new to accessibility it can be hard to exactly understand what it is and what you are trying to achieve. It may seem slightly abstract, unobtainable, and difficult to grasp fully. This is understandable. There are aspects of accessibility that are easier to understand than others, but with time, as things come into focus, you will learn that accessibility is rather practical. It is made up of real world problems, for real users, and with tangible solutions.

I think of accessibility as a continuum. It is an ever-evolving line. I found this to be a very helpful mental picture when I was trying to understand accessibility.

If you build websites, write software, design user interfaces, or produce any electronic content, then what you design and build, code and write, is somewhere on that line. If you imagine that line as one that moves and grows, then your position on that line is also always in flux—always changing as what you design evolves.

This is largely because technology is always changing. As you read further and hopefully understand more about people with disabilities and users of assistive technology (AT), you will see that there are some core issues for each user group that don't really change even if the technology does. For example, you will see that blind users need to access equivalent content that tells them what a particular image is all about; or that people with limited physical mobility would really appreciate not having a lot of useless links to tab through in order to get to the content that you have placed at the bottom of the page, and so on.

On the other hand, the technology that people use to access the Web is also constantly developing and changing as the Web evolves. This brings challenges for everyone—the developer or author, the vendor of assistive technology (AT), the browser manufacturer and the people who draw up future specifications of the coding languages that the Web is built on. So all of these elements are related, and they are also always in a state of flux. Therefore, I think the continuum analogy is a useful one.

So it's not really good to think, "Oh, I am here now. I know all there is to know", or "My interfaces are perfect and my code rocks". While there may be degrees of truth in these statements and if you know what you are doing, by all means be confident about what you design, but please remember that there is always room for improvement.

 Accessibility is in many ways a 'quality' issue and therefore good accessible interfaces, applications and websites are therefore a useful by-product of good design and development practices.

Usability

Usability looks at the quality of the user experience and tries to determine how successfully a user can complete a task and how satisfying a device or interface is to use. Including usability in your workflow is also a very important part of good designing and development.

Areas where user interaction can be improved therefore come under usability. While usability and accessibility (strictly speaking) are different disciplines, there are close connections and crossovers between them.

Following are some definitions of usability picked from some good websites:

"A measure of how easy it is for a user to complete a task. In the context of Web pages this concerns how easy it is for a user to find the information they require from a given Web site."

"The ease with which a system can be learnt or used. A figure of merit or qualitative judgment of ease of use or learning. Some methods of assessing usability may also express usability as a quantitative index."

"The effectiveness, efficiency, and satisfaction with which specified users can achieve specified goals in a particular environment. Synonymous with 'ease of use'."

I have included several definitions, as there are some related points I would like to make. As I mentioned, accessibility and usability are two different fields, but there is a very strong relationship between the two. The first definition focuses on the user's ability to complete the task. That is obviously very important. So being able to successfully complete a task is an important part of usability, and, I am sure you will agree, good design in general.

The second definition is interesting as it mentions how easily the system can be 'learnt'. A good rule of thumb in user interface design is to provide instructions on how to perform particular tasks. The user should just 'get it'. This is, of course in some situations, impossible. The user won't just 'get' how to fly a plane for example, but I am sure that you have come across web interfaces that you quickly just 'knew' how to use. It just 'felt right'. This is what I am getting at.

The third definition is one of the most interesting as it goes beyond dryly looking at the 'tasks' the user needs to do and mentions the level of satisfaction the users will feel when they use a web interface. This is really important and takes the usability definition to a higher level by looking at the quality of the user experience and not merely a task-based approach. This is something that I would like you to consider when you build your websites. Not merely the dry completion of tasks but the quality of the user experience, especially for people with disabilities.

Donald Norman, one of the daddies of usability, mentions the following on his website:

> "*I caution that logical analysis is not a good way to predict people's behavior (nor are focus groups or surveys): observation is the key. I caution that the time frame for adoption of new technologies is measured in decades, not the months everyone would prefer. And I help formulate new products and services. For both products and services I'm a champion of beauty, pleasure and fun, coupled with behavioral and functional effectiveness.*"

I like Donald's books and highly recommend them.

While usability is related to the creation of accessible content, some may say it is a lateral relationship. There may be a suggestion that as disciplines they are not connected at all. However, for me they are not mutually exclusive and should not be considered so.

Usability is about looking at how usable, intuitive, user friendly, and satisfying an interface is to use. As a discipline, it examines the psychology of user interaction. It is an attempt to understand how users perceive the instructions they receive from looking at, or interacting with, a user interface or device. Also understanding what the designer is trying to achieve, and how this can be translated in something that works and that people are happy to use; or even pay for, or buy.

When you design your site, some useful information can be gathered by your own intuitive sense of how usable your designs are. Listen to your intuition; it's there for a reason. Trusting your instincts for what you feel would be both good and bad for your design and development practices can really pay off.

User Testing

User testing is where you get users with varying levels of ability to use your website. These tests can be videoed and analyzed later, and help to give everyone involved in the project a good idea of what works and what doesn't.

Involving users in the design process like this is a great thing to do. It is using technology in an inclusive way to increase the quality of the web interfaces, and it truly democratizes technology, creating a level playing field for everyone.

There may be user testing facilities in your area that you could use, and it is worthwhile getting someone who has experience of running user tests and other aspects of usability to do this for you. They know what to look for and can advise you about improving your website's design based on the feedback they get from the test.

I have been very fortunate to have been able to set up a fully professional user testing lab, with my colleague Mark Magennis, in the National Council for the Blind of Ireland, where I work. The lab also has a separate observation room, where people can remotely view the tests. The lab has been very successful and has helped many developers really understand accessibility and the importance of usability in their projects.

 User testing is a very powerful way of producing high quality websites. It also takes accessibility off the platform of merely being an intellectual or theoretical exercise.

Using Personas

If user testing is not possible then what else can you do in order to simulate real world use of your site for your users? This is where using personas can be useful.

A persona is like a distilled archetype of user groups. This is a fancy way of saying you make a model of what you think an average user from a particular group would be like and you build a persona around them.

The idea is that if the various personas are accurate, so will be your simulation of their experience, and you can then modify your design around as per their needs are and experiences of each persona.

Building Personas

Personas are created from the research you do about your target group, this can be from surveys, interviews and so on. You then build imaginary personas that represent an average user. These various groups can include older people, young people, blind users, and so on.

While it is fairly easy to get your head around what a persona is, putting it all together can be daunting. The level of detail you wish to get into is up to you but the more 'real' you make a persona the better the result will be. A good persona come from real world feedback that you have gathered.

Understanding Accessibility

You may have your own knowledge and experience of accessibility. This could range from little, to a lot. It could be based on your experience, things you have read during your own research, or stuff that you have picked up from colleagues and fellow developers based on their experience and research.

You may not know any people with disabilities or any people who use assistive technology (AT). Much of what you have heard could come from second or third hand information that could either be wrong, or worse, misleading.

You may have downloaded a demo copy of a screen reader and realized that it a very complex piece of software that you can't just hop into and drive off with. Well, not smoothly anyway.

You may have read about certain assistive technology and are trying to picture in your mind how it may work. I am aware that this approach is very difficult. If it is possible for you to gain some hands-on being experience of being with people with disabilities and watch how they can use technology, even for only an hour or two, I think you would find it very useful.

You will see how helpful the technology can be in their lives, and it will hopefully make it clearer why you need to spend time learning how to build accessible interfaces. You can do this by contacting your local disability services, and asking them if you could drop into their centre or talk to some users of assistive technology within the organization. I am sure they will be glad to help you.

Being Accessible Doesn't Hurt

Accessibility is an area that many developers can feel forced into due to the legislative changes, business pressures, etc. and is often something that they really don't want to be bothered about. I completely understand.

When coupled with complex technical specifications and obscure guidelines it can seem to be a Herculean task, and this is when you have just started understanding accessibility. What I hope to do is to break down some core things, and if you pay attention to them, I am confident that you will create more accessible websites in no time, without having to take on a PhD in the process.

What I wish to do, is help you to get the grip with two or three core areas, which will make your sites more usable and accessible to the widest range of users, including people with disabilities.

WCAG 1.0

The WCAG (Web Content Accessibility Guidelines) are an important set of guidelines and techniques that outline important areas to pay particular attention to when developing accessible websites. By following the guidelines and successfully passing their various checkpoints or success criteria, you will have gone a long way towards creating more accessible websites.

In this book I have chosen not to give you guidance on 'how to comply with WCAG', rather I have distilled my experience and covered many of the important areas, which when followed will serve the need of many of your users. You may also, happily, comply with many parts of the WCAG guidelines.

There are two sets of WCAG guidelines (version 1.0 and version 2.0). WCAG version 2.0 is still in draft. However, you could start reading version 1.0, but do keep an eye on the newer version which I have outlined next. The new guidelines are a major improvement and a promising evolution. They are not perfect but hey, evolution is messy but necessary.

WCAG 2.0 is still in draft as I write this in the second half of 2007. However, even if some of the details of the current draft change, I doubt that they will change much and much of what is in the current draft is, in principle, a good piece of advice.

Differences Between WCAG 1.0 and WCAG 2.0

Techniques that you pick up from version 1.0 will not be 'inaccessible' or fail version 2.0, but bear in mind that the WCAG 1.0 guidelines are older (from the last century), and things have moved on. While in some ways the differences between the two are superficial, in other more important ways they are profound.

As you will see shortly WCAG 1.0 had various priority checkpoints, WCAG 2.0 has 'success criteria'. While WCAG 1.0 was organized around a set of guidelines, WCAG 2.0 is organized around four principles.

WCAG 2.0 applies to a much broader range of technologies than WCAG 1.0, and is much more testable. In fact success in WCAG 2.0 hangs on each 'success criteria' being testable. WCAG 2.0 has far more extensive guidelines with detailed techniques available to ensure conformance.

WCAG 2.0 is more applicable to the many existing technologies that are around today, non W3C technologies, and future technologies.

One of the things that I really like about WCAG 2.0 is that it is organized around some sound principles. These are four simple principles and are grouped under the acronym **POUR**.

Principle 1—Content Must be Perceivable (P)

This refers to all the content including Multimedia, Video and Audio.

- Provide an alternative text for all the non-text content.
- Synchronized alternatives for Multimedia (captioned video, audio descriptions, etc.).
- Information and structure must be separate from presentation.
- Make it easy to distinguish foreground information from background. (Good Color contrast).

Principle 2—Interface Elements must be Operable (O)

- All the functionalities must be operable via the keyboard.
- Users must control limits on their reading or interaction.
- Users must be able to avoid content that can cause seizures due to photosensitivity.
- Provide mechanisms for users to find content, orientate themselves and navigate through it.
- Help users avoid mistakes and make it easier to correct mistakes when they do occur.

Principle 3—Content and Controls must be Understandable (U)

- Make text content readable and understandable.
- Make the placement and functionality of content predictable.

Principle 4—Content Should be Robust Enough to Work with Current and Future Technologies (R)

- Support compatibility with current and future user agents.
- Ensure that content is accessible or provide accessible alternatives.

While WCAG 1.0 was not perfect and in many ways outdated quickly as the Web rapidly changed; it is hoped that WCAG 2.0 will successfully fill in the gaps and be somewhat future proof.

Understanding WCAG

When I first came across WCAG 1.0, I remember my head hurting after reading just one or two paragraphs. They seemed to be nearly indecipherable cabalistic codes written in a language that was itself, quite inaccessible.

Another big problem that I also felt that it was very difficult to establish a 'hierarchy of importance' from the WCAG 1.0. I wish to say that this was not the author's fault, as the guidelines are prioritized, but I just didn't 'get it'. Well, not easily anyway. So I used to wonder "What's vital and what is, nice to have?" and I was left with no 'real' sense of this much needed 'hierarchy of importance'. I did not have any contacts with people who had disabilities or other developers who had the experience to guide me.

There are also some important limitations in WCAG 1.0. Many of the Priority 3 checkpoints are highly subjective and the priority system itself was skewed, some of the AAA (least important) should be AA and some AA should be A (very important), etc.

Summary

While accessibility is very important it is not the full picture when it comes to a good user-interface design and there are other important aspects to be considered such as usability. For me, accessibility and usability make up a powerful combination for a potent holistic approach to web development and a positive user experience for everyone.

User testing is a really practical way of determining whether your sites are not only accessible but also usable, and this important method for qualitative analysis really does lift accessibility and usability out of the arena of being merely a theoretical or academic exercise.

User testing can really give you positive proof that all of your hard work—in getting to the point where you can say that your interfaces are accessible and usable—has really paid off.

Regarding WCAG, much of what is suggested in the WCAG guidelines is in many ways common sense, if you give it some thought. What I hope to do is provide you with a step-by-step way of creating a WCAG compliant website using Joomla! I will focus in the rest of the book on what I feel are some of the main areas that you should give your attention to. By doing so, you will be in a better position to develop more accessible and usable websites and interfaces.

3

Understanding Disability and Assistive Technology (AT)

In this chapter, I will share a few of disabilities types and how users with these disabilities could use technology.

I also understand how difficult it would be for you to successfully design and build accessible websites for users with varying degrees of abilities, especially if you have no experience of interacting with people who have disabilities. It can seem like a tall order, and in many ways it is. However, I hope that this chapter will help you to understand some aspects of disability. At the very least I hope that you will understand how diverse we as a species really are.

Blindness

There are many different degrees of blindness. I work for the National Council for the Blind of Ireland and most of our services are for visually impaired users and not users who are completely blind.

For example, a friend of mine can see perfectly well, but has a very rare and extreme form of dyslexia and is legally registered blind. He cannot read, or remember, or understand symbols, as he has a very short term memory, but he can 'see'. However, he is still considered blind for all intents and purposes. So, if a person is considered blind, it does not mean that he or she cannot see anything at all.

Some blind users may be able to make out some degrees of light and dark, shapes, and other forms, others may not be able to see anything at all. People who are new to assistive technology (AT) and accessibility are usually quite shocked and surprised when they discover that there are many successful blind people working in the IT industry. I know some truly great nerds who are completely blind! Later in this chapter, I will discuss how blind people can successfully use computers.

Visual Impairment

There are a wide range of visual impairments. I have included some photographic examples here, which simulate some of the more common conditions. They will give you some idea of what the vision of a person with conditions like glaucoma, macular degeneration, etc. can be like.

Following screenshots are of a user getting on a bus in Dublin.

Glaucoma

The following shows a Glaucoma visual sample:

A person with glaucoma may experience loss of their peripheral or side vision. In the early stage glaucoma causes a subtle loss of contrast, which can lead to difficulties seeing things around your environment and certainly lead to difficulty using a computer monitor.

This can lead to what is called 'tunnel vision' where the person can still read and do close-up work but has no side vision.

Macular Degeneration

The following shows a Macular degeneration visual sample:

This condition is quite common amongst older people and causes a loss of vision in the centre of the eye. Reading, writing and up-close work can become very difficult. A person may encounter problems in identifying colors.

Retinopathy

The following shows a Retinopathy visual sample:

This condition causes a partial blurring of vision or patchy loss of vision and can be brought on by advanced diabetes. The person's near vision may be reduced; they may have difficulty with reading up close.

Detached Retina

The following shows a detached retina visual sample:

A detached retina can result in a loss of vision where the retina has been damaged. A detached retina may appear like a dark shadow over part of the eye or the person may experience bright flashes of light or showers of dark spots.

Physical Disabilities

There are many kinds of physical disabilities. Some of them can be quite extreme. Physical disabilities can manifest in such a broad range of ways for many reasons. People can be born with physical disabilities or acquire them later in life due to an accident or old age.

Common mobility problems include tremors, shakes, becoming easily exhausted, or experiencing difficulty in movement. Many people with physical disabilities cannot use a mouse at all and therefore have great difficulty if websites are not keyboard accessible. In fact, ensuring your website is keyboard accessible is probably one of the greatest things you can do to help users with physical disabilities.

Cognitive Disabilities

The term 'Cognitive disability' is a broad term that includes users who have difficulty with mental tasks. This can cover issues with solving problems, memory and attention, understanding language, and so on.

Of all the disabilities, users with cognitive disabilities are probably the most difficult to accommodate. It is such a new field, particularly in its relation to the Web, that methods of accommodating this user groups' needs are still being developed. In short, it is hard to find definitive evidence of what does and doesn't work.

However, use of good and clear design and site layout, intuitive information architecture, simple interfaces and language in your website are useful techniques which will help. Indeed, you can use these rules of thumb to not only help users with cognitive disabilities, but every one else as well!

Assistive Technology (AT)

There are many kinds of assistive technologies and there are also many definitions. I like this one from the US National Multiple Sclerosis Society:

> *"A term used to describe all of the tools, products, and devices, from the simplest to the most complex, that can make a particular function easier or possible to perform."*

Note that it doesn't mention disability at all, and I think this is also important. We don't really think of our spectacles or our TV remote controls as assistive technology, but they are. I like the idea of technology that can be used by many different people regardless of their abilities; technology that is not just used by people with disabilities but by the ordinary user who doesn't think of themselves as being disabled, but is just using a technology because it works really well. This takes AT out of the 'disability only' sector and makes it more inclusive, or at least our perception about it.

 For a humourous and fun introduction to AT check out the AT boogie video by Jeff Moyer with animation by Haik Hoisington at: `http://www.inclusive.com/AT_boogie/at30.swf`

As I mentioned in my introduction, I appreciate that many of you will not have direct experience using AT, know what AT is, or know any people with disabilities, so it's not unreasonable to say that being asked to design and create web interfaces to serve these needs is definitely a tall order. I hope that the following will help somewhat in giving you a brief introduction to what various AT is all about, help to shed some light on how people with disabilities use these great technologies, and how you, as a website developer, can help to ensure that their user experience was a pleasant one.

What is a Screen Reader?

A screen reader is text-to-speech software that literally reads out the contents of the screen to a user, whether it's a web page, a structured MS Word document, or even a tagged PDF. Screen readers can also interact very well with the operating system of the computer itself and can give a blind user a deep level of interaction, allowing the performance of complex system administration tasks. Screen readers are mostly used by blind and visually impaired people, but they can also be used by other user groups who find them useful, like people with dyslexia.

There are many different screen readers available like JAWS (`http://www.freedomscientific.com/fs_products/JAWS_HQ.asp`), Window-Eyes (`http://www.gwmicro.com/Window-Eyes/`), the free open source Linux screen reader ORCA (`http://live.gnome.org/Orca`), and the free NVDA (`http://www.nvda-project.org/`), as well as the very promising VoiceOver (`http://www.apple.com/accessibility/voiceover/`), which comes bundled with Mac OS X. Some screen readers like JAWS can be very expensive pieces of software.

It is important to note that when you design and develop your sites, you don't design and code for a particular screen reader or other assistive technology.

There are core principles that we will discuss in this book that will benefit all screen reader users regardless of the brand or platform. Much of what we will discuss will be under the remit of what are called 'Web Standards' (http://en.wikipedia.org/wiki/Web_standards), which can be though of as embodying best practice in web design and development.

So I don't suggest, "Oh mark up something like this because it works a certain way with JAWS." Or "If I code like this, a Window-Eyes user will be able to do this", and so on. The ideal is that the specification of a language like HTML or XHTML will be well designed and then the vendors (who make the software) will support the well-designed specification, which will lead to an inclusive Web that is accessible to everyone. That's the idea.

Screen Magnification

A screen magnification software allows the user to literally view their desktop or web browser at an increased rate of magnification. This feature is already a part of the Windows operating system and Mac OS X. The difference between a dedicated package and the feature in your operating system is of quality and clarity; this is obviously important for users with poor vision.

When you use the magnification features of your operating system you can get artifacts and blurred text whereas a screen magnification package like Supernova or Zoomtext will redraw the screen at a high resolution and they have other features, which provide high quality anti-aliasing, therefore the re-drawn text is sharper and clearer.

Switch Access

Enhanced informational design is also good for users with limited physical mobility or movement. Users with physical disabilities often use a device called a **switch** to interact with their computer and access the Web. The following figure shows large single button switches:

The following screenshots show a variety of switches:

A switch is often a single large button designed so that the user can easily press it with the least amount of effort.

There are switches that can be controlled, not by pressing them but by blowing into them, or by wobbling them, and a host of other forms of tactile interaction designed to suit the ability of the user.

Some users will use a combination of two or more of these switches, each of which can be set to perform a different task or represent a certain input. This can greatly increase the user's power and speed of interaction with the computer or web interface. However, some users with very limited movement may successfully use only one button to interact, browse the web, type emails and other documents or play games.

How Do Switches Work?

Switches are usually used in conjunction with **scanning software** applications such as the Grid (`http://www.mkprosopsis.com/Software/The%20Grid.htm`), Clicker (`http://www.cricksoft.com/us/products/clicker/`), and EZKeys (`http://www.words-plus.com/website/products/soft/ezkeysxp.htm`). These are used by people who may have had a stroke or other physical disabilities, which results in limited or uncontrollable movement, like cerebral palsy. The user's disability may also mean that the user may not have much control over their movement or they may have involuntary spasms that can make using a traditional mouse or keyboard very difficult, and in some cases, impossible to operate.

These scanning packages work by dividing the screen into a grid type layout and highlighting the content of the grid one square at a time. This temporary highlighting happens in a linear fashion and is referred to as scanning. When the user wishes to select the content of the square they can press the switch button. The following figures show the grid interface

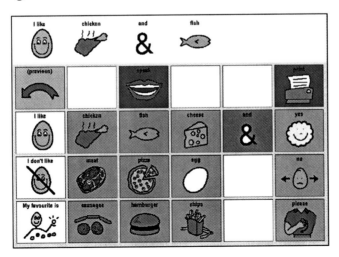

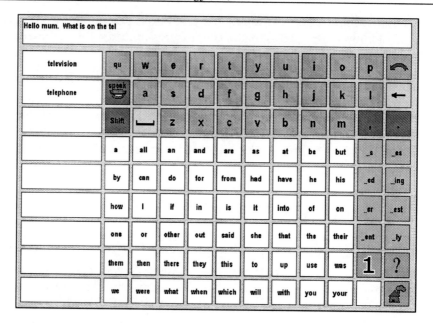

This powerful combination of single or multiple switch and grid type software is an empowering technology for people with disabilities; enabling them to use their computers, communicate with family and friends via email, and surf the Web.

Mouse Emulation

Another scanning-type application that operates a little differently is EZ Keys XP. EZ Keys XP provides complete mouse emulation using alternative inputs, such as a keyboard or even a slight movement of the eye using switch activation. It has several access modes, including standard keyboard, expanded keyboard, joystick and single and multiple switch scanning.

EZ Keys has useful features such as an 'Instant Phrase editor' where there are many pre-made or custom made phrases that can be easily recalled and used as needed, either by copying them and pasting into e-mail clients or by speaking them out.

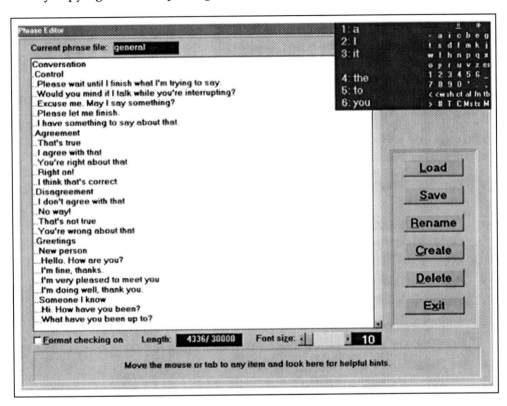

 Paying attention to your site layout and reducing the number of clicks or complex menus that users have to wade through to get to content is a great help to many users of these kinds of assistive technologies.

Useful Tools for Developers

There are some very useful tools developers can easily add to their browser in order to help with the development of accessible websites, as well as simulating the experience someone with a disability may have when they are online.

A few of them are as follows:

Web Accessibility Tools Consortium (WAT-C)

The Web Accessibility Tools Consortium (WAT-C) provides a collection of free tools to assist both the developers and designers in the development and testing of accessible web content. The consortium is a collaboration of some of the world's leading accessibility practitioners, founded by Accessible Information Solutions (AIS Australia), Infoaxia (Japan), The Paciello Group (USA), Wrong HTML (Japan), and Juicy Studio (UK).

There are several very interesting projects that WAT-C members have initiated, contributed to or been a part of. They include the following:

- The Web Accessibility Toolbar (Version 1 and 2). Available in English, French and Italian.
- The Contrast Analyser 2.0. The Contrast Analyser 2.0 implements the updated contrast algorithm and provides results based on Guideline 1.4 of the May 2007 working draft of WCAG 2.0.
- A Colour Contrast Analyser for MAC.
- The Web Accessibility Toolbar for Opera (WAT for Opera) 1.1
- Web Developer Extension—Japanese & Korean localizations of Chris Pederick's extension for Mozilla/Firefox.
- All these can be accessed via the WAT-C website at: http://www.wat-c.org/

Mozilla Web Developer Toolbar

Chris Pederick developed this truly great tool and I highly recommend it if you are a Firefox user. The Web developer toolbar includes various development tools such as window resizing, form and image debugging, links to page validation and optimization tools, and much more.

You can get it at:

http://chrispederick.com/work/web-developer/

It has tons of features that you will find useful in assessing the accessibility of the websites that you build with Joomla! as well as any other websites that you choose.

Patrick H. Lauke also wrote a really useful article on how using Mozilla Firefox with the Web Developer toolbar can help with the various manual checks of WCAG 1.0. You can read at:

```
http://www.ariadne.ac.uk/issue44/lauke/
```

Patrick takes you through each of the guidelines and demonstrates how you can use the toolbar to check for areas where there has been both success and failure in your websites in compliance with WCAG 1.0. It also allows you to quickly examine the parts of your code that could do with a dust off and improvements in general.

 Much of what Patrick discusses will be equally as relevant for WCAG 2.0 and the tool will be useful in helping you to achieve compliance with the new version of the guidelines as it was in with WCAG 1.0.

Another useful extension for Firefox is 'Fangs'. It is a screen reader emulator. That means it doesn't talk but gives you a text representation of the expected output from a webpage and how a screen reader would output it. You can get it at:

```
http://sourceforge.net/projects/fangs
```

Sitting Comfortably? Then we'll Begin

Now that you know a little bit more about different kinds of disabilities, the various AT available to help users browse the Internet, and some useful tools for you as a developer. I would like you to try the following exercises as well. I hope that it will help you to further understand what it is like to browse the Internet in a restricted fashion and maybe then you can gain a deeper understanding of what it will be like for people with disabilities when they go online.

These exercises are a poor substitute for interacting directly with people with disabilities and talking to them about their experiences, but I hope you find them useful anyway.

I call the first exercise "No Frills" browsing.

Exercise 1—"No Frills" Browsing

The idea behind "No Frills" browsing is that you will try to emulate the experience that people with disabilities may have when they go online. The purpose of the exercise is to get you to think about the common barriers that people with disabilities often face when they are online.

For example, disabling images in your browser is useful for you to understand the importance of suitable alt text—if no accessible equivalents exist and the image contains a lot of useful information—that you will just not see when you browse with images off, or if you are blind.

The following steps are a guide only and you may, of course, vary them as you feel.

Many of the settings that you need to change will be in the Preferences section of your browser. They may be 'Internet Options' or something similar. However, you may use something like the AIS accessibility toolbar or the Mozilla Web Developer Toolbars mentioned earlier to make this exercise easier. Whatever way you choose to modify your browser, these are the main areas that you should concentrate on.

I would like you to turn off the following

- Style Sheets
- Images
- Sound
- JavaScript
- Java
- Support for Flash

If You are Using Firefox

If you are not using any of the toolbars (though I hope you do try them), disabling many of these features in Firefox is made rather easy. The following is a screen shot from the **Preferences** dialogue box.

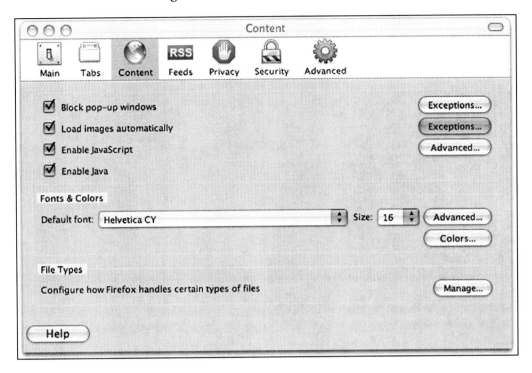

Unselecting **Load images automatically, Enable JavaScript** and **Enable Java** will effectively do all we need for a successful 'No Frills" browsing experience.

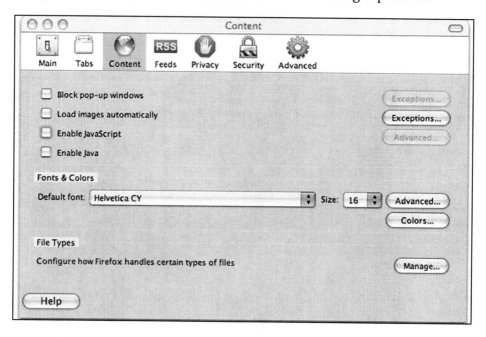

Deactivating the **Block pop-up Windows** feature is also a useful thing to try because in accessibility terms using pop-ups is not a good idea and should be avoided where possible.

 Pop-up windows can be annoying not only for sighted users; they can have a stronger negative impact on people with disabilities have when they encounter them; especially users with limited mobility and those with cognitive disabilities.

Pop-ups can also be disorientating for non-visual users depending on what they have been used for. For example, at the very least blind users often find that they have to toggle between the page they are on and the pop-up page. For the advanced users this may not be a problem, but you should not design your site only for them.

If the user really needs to access some widget or search function contained in the pop-up page in order to properly use the site—it gets even messier.

Pop-ups exist in the gray area between being an accessibility issue and a usability issue. I hope that you will realize as you read this book that there are several such gray areas between accessibility and usability. While they are separate disciplines, they are closely intertwined and not mutually exclusive.

In short, don't use pop-ups, or spawning windows. Don't even link to external sites in new browser windows—if you can at all avoid it. Not without, at the very least, informing the user that this is going to happen.

Internet Explorer

If you are using Internet Explorer, changing its functionality can be a bit fiddly. This is why I recommend that you download the AIS toolbar and use it in your work as it can really help.

IE 7 also has the new pop-up blocker feature that can be easily activated via **Tools ->Pop-up Blocker**.

To disable scripting and other features, go to **Tools -> Internet Options** and select **Security**, then **Custom Level**. In the **Security Settings** dialogue box, you will have several options and it can be a headache figuring out which is which. I will try to give you an overview here.

ActiveX

ActiveX is a Microsoft technology used for developing reusable object-oriented software components. ActiveX is an alternate name for OLE automation, and not a separate technology. It is similar to a Java Applet, but it only runs in a Windows environment; it cannot be considered cross platform. ActiveX controls are used to build plug-ins for IE.

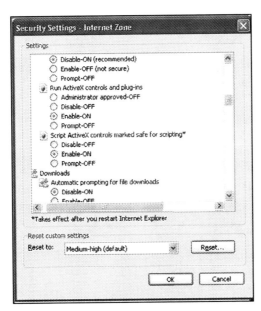

It can be useful to disable ActiveX controls and plug-ins and see if your site is still accessible. However, this will probably have very little impact if your site contains no video or embedded rich media content like Flash, or basically any elements that may require ActiveX to be enabled in order for them to function or be served to your browser.

There are some issues with how Flash content gets embedded into the browser such as ActiveX controls trapping focus. This is where the user cannot tab out of a Flash movie using ActiveX Controls.

Whereas in the past there were some issues of earlier screen reader incompatibility with ActiveX controls, and some DHTML events are disabled when ActiveX is off so this may also interfere with some AJAX type widgets or WAI-ARIA Live Regions. However, I have not encountered any noteworthy ActiveX meltdowns over the past couple of years but please do experiment with the settings in your browser.

Disabling JavaScript and Java in IE

To disable JavaScript and Java in IE 5/6/7, in the **Security Settings** dialogue box, scroll down to the **Scripting section,** and click **Disable** under **Active scripting** and **Scripting of Java applets.** This will effectively take care of both for the purposes of our 'No Frills' exercise.

Flash content

Finally disable any Flash content. You may need a third party plug-in to do this. If you are using IE you could try 'Flashswitch':

http://www.flashswitch.com/

If you are using Firefox have a look at the Firefox extension 'Flashblock':

https://addons.mozilla.org/en-US/firefox/addon/433

Another useful Firefox extension that I really like is 'NoScript'. I use it myself (as I always browse with JavaScript disabled). It uses what it calls 'Whitelist based preemptive script blocking', which means that you basically load every site with Javascript off. Java and Flash also remain off if you so choose. You then select the sites that you will let run these scripts on and other content by adding them to your Whitelist as you go.

For more on NoScript see:

http://noscript.net/

Mouse Free Zone

Ok, so you have, one way or the other, modified your browser. Now what do you do? If you think that you have gotten off lightly, think again! I want you to abandon your mouse. Yup. Plug it out. Throw it away to be dramatic and have that sense of no going back—if you like—but whatever you do don't reach for it while you are in 'No Frills' mode.

Soon you will have a taste of what the Web is really like for many users, like those who rely on the keyboard alone to navigate online. This will hopefully also hammer home how important it is for the Web interfaces that you design to be keyboard accessible.

The Acid Test

In order for the test to work, it is important that you pick a few tasks to do with each of the sites that you visit. There are no hard and fast rules about how many sites you choose to visit. In fact one site that you are used to and can perform a real world task such as buying something, writing a blog post, or adding some kind of rich media content to, are all representative of good tasks to try. Why not do each of these and see what else you come up with?

By browsing sites that you are familiar with, you will get a totally fresh perspective on the user experience of people with disabilities. In some ways it will be like starting over. If you look at your own sites and try this test you will maybe get a shock, especially if you are new to accessibility. If you do get a fright, I hope that it is short and not too sharp, but enough to get you thinking about how to improve your development methods and design practices.

Finally—Was It Good for You?

So what was it like? Was it as you expected? Was it easier or harder than you thought it would be to perform the various tasks you set for yourself? Or are you glad it's over and do you desperately want to return your browser to normal as soon as possible?

There are many responses to this experience and you will probably be a little fried after it and cannot wait to get things back, the way you like them.

Try it yourself

I hope you find the "No Frills" exercise really useful and that you test the sites you build with Joomla! using the 'No Frills' method.

Testing your sites in this way will help you show where you have got your developments right and the areas where you need to improve. The good news is that it is possible to accommodate many different types of disabilities and methods of user interaction; the 'No Frills' exercise can also help to show you what you got right.

Remember – what you have experienced here is only a fraction of the frustration and annoyance many people with disabilities experience when they use badly designed, inaccessible websites.

Exercise 2—Turn Off Your Display

I will not recommend this exercise to novice coders and developers, however some of you may find it useful. However, "caveat emptor", as it requires a steely determination to get to learn how to use a screen reader properly!

Download a demo copy of JAWS (PC only), or some other free screen reader, like ORCA or NVDA. JAWS demo's can be easily found at the Freedom Scientific website.

The demo copy of JAWS will last – fully functioning for 40 minutes – before closing down, if you wish to use it again just reboot your machine.

This time restriction does have the advantage that when you start learning you can spend 40 minute slots working with and studying how to use JAWS, and then take a little break if it all gets too much.

The reason I am saying that this exercise may not be suitable is because screen readers are rather complex applications that have a very steep learning curve, particularly if you don't have to use them. Using screen readers can be difficult, tricky and frustrating. You have been warned. If you're not fazed by this then this is what I want you to do.

Firstly, download the demo version of the software and install it on your PC. Then read the manual, or at least the introductory parts such as keyboard strokes, etc. Practice regularly and you will hopefully reach a point where you feel you are fairly confident using it; remember that this may take some practice. You can also seek help and advice from your local services for blind and visually impaired users in your area.

Once you are comfortable and confident with this then find some websites, turn off your monitor and try and use them. This can be very effective for sites that you already know, as you will see them from a very different perspective. Also it's useful for task-orientated site visits as well as general browsing. What I mean is before you visit a site, define some tasks that you would like to carry out when you are there, such as booking concert tickets, a flight or buying some books; then try and carry these tasks out with your monitor off using the screen reader software.

Now try out the screen reader on your own sites that you build using Joomla!

Be patient. It took me well over a year before I became proficient using a screen reader and I had the advantage of working for a charity that provides services to blind and visually impaired people. So go easy on yourself and if you do make progress you will find it very useful.

What is interesting about this exercise is there are varying levels of competence among the blind and visually impaired screen reader users. Not all screen reader users are power users and a few use some very basic functionality that the screen reader actually has.

Summary

In this chapter we looked at various types of disabilities as well as the variety of assistive technologies that are available. We also looked at how you can modify your browsing experience in order to try and gain a greater understanding of what it is like for people with disabilities when they go online.

We also looked at various tools you can use with your browser and some fun 'No Frills' exercises. In the next chapter we will look at the various techniques screen reader users have at their disposal when they access online content.

4
Creating Accessible Content

In this chapter we are going to look at some of the nuts and bolts of creating accessible content. We will also look at some basic HTML code with a quick and simple refresher that I hope you will find useful.

In this chapter we will be rolling up our sleeves and getting under the hood with Joomla!. We will be looking at the following areas:

- Using headings and other HTML elements to provide content structure
- Providing alternative text to images
- Using descriptive link text to assist accessibility
- Using tables and how to mark them up appropriately

Describe What it is, Not How it Looks

We often format a piece of written content by changing the way it looks. For example, we may increase a heading's font size so it looks prominent and important, or highlight the text with a bright color or use **bold** or *italics* for emphasis.

So how do you describe the importance of these big headings or imply expressions like emphasis to someone who cannot see? One of the most important rules when creating accessible content is to describe *what the text means* in terms of importance, not just how it looks. Leave how it looks to the template designer (and if you are the template designer, then leave it until the next chapter!).

So how do you describe what something is or what it means, rather than just how it looks? How can you make a browser, interpret that meaning correctly? This is what HTML does very well.

One of the first things you learn when you build accessible websites is that you should separate the structure (which describes what a piece of content is) from style (which describes how different types of content should look).

In the following sections, we will see how to use the Joomla! content editor to indicate what the text means in structural terms, so that all the users can benefit from this information and not the just users who can see.

All the (X)HTML You Need in Two Minutes

All the text content in a web page is sent to the browser as *plain text*, with some extra information to tell the browser how to format the various elements. The browser makes a decision on how to present the text to the user based on that extra information. This extra information is called **HTML** or **XHTML** (in the two minutes we have, you don't need to know the difference between the two — we will stick with HTML).

You can think of the web browser as an actor. He or she is given a script by the director (that's you when you write your web page) that contains the dialogues (which is the content), and some extra notes on how to say them (which is the HTML).

In this HTML script these notes are all put into angle brackets, so that they don't get mixed with the content. An instruction or HTML element inside angle brackets is often called a *tag*.

Simple elements include `<h1>` for 'major heading', `<p>` for 'paragraph', `<ol>` for 'ordered (i.e. numbered) list', and `<blockquote>` for 'a paragraph that quotes what someone says'. You can also reference a website by using the `cite` attribute, which is an attribute of the `<blockquote>` element. As you read further you will see that many HTML elements have different attributes, which can be thought of as properties or qualities. For example, water (which is an also an element!) has qualities like being wet, or can used to drink, or water your plants, or fire (another element!), which has properties of being hot or providing light.

The following example formats an imaginary section of my website, as a `<blockquote>`.

```
<BLOCKQUOTE cite="http://www.cfit.ie/quotes/quote_of_the_day.html">
<P>So blockquote can be used to tell the browser that this piece of
text has been written by the persons cited by the cite attribute</P>
</BLOCKQUOTE>
```

You will notice that if you try this in your own browser you will not see the contents of the cite attribute at all.

All these examples describe 'what the content is'.

There are other elements in HTML that describe how the content should look. The most notorious of these is <font>, which specifies the typeface, size, and color. It has now deprecated, which is just another way of saying, don't use it anymore as there are now better ways to do the same thing; in this case using CSS.

So HTML has loads of different elements that you use to describe what the content is and doing this helps to turn your content into accessible content so the user agents like the screen reader or browser—like all good actors—can interpret these instructions in a way that's suitable for its audience.

Using Headings to Communicate Structure

The most important thing about the 'what this content is' tags are the headings.

A heading in HTML has a special meaning particularly for people using assistive technology (AT). Don't think that increasing the font size and changing the typeface is an OK alternative to using proper headings. Making your fonts bold or increasing the font size is only skin deep. Instead, make sure you use headings appropriately.

We'll see how to use headings appropriately in a moment, but first we need to find some content to experiment on.

Time For Action—Let's Add Some Content

When I put together some example for this book—which are some articles on Music—I divided them into four sections, Classical Music, Funk, Reggae and Soul. I took some articles from Wikipedia to use as content, as looking at endless streams of "Lorem ipsum dolor sit amet etc", soon gets a bit old.

So that's what you will see in the following examples. The text came preformatted with links, so it may look a little different from what you do with Joomla! but I don't want you to worry about it when you look at the following screenshots.

The methods I show you are sound and will work with any content.

The following screenshots show what the Tiny MCE editor pane in the new article section looks like with no content:

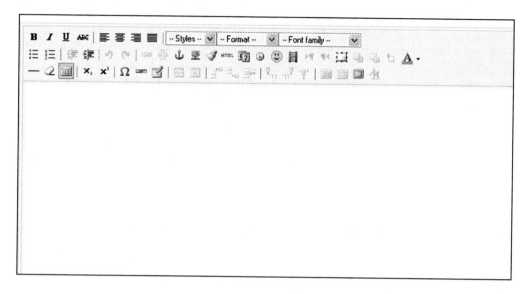

1. Go to the application that you are using to write your content.

2. Select the text you wish to insert into Joomla! and copy it (*Ctrl + C*) from a Word file or similar (depending on what you are working with) and paste it on the clipboard.

3. When you have copied the text, move back to Joomla! Click on the WYSIWYG editor pane where you wish to insert the content. If this is a fresh page it will be in the top left or thereabouts.

4. Paste the contents from the clipboard into the editor (*Ctrl + V*).

What Just Happened?

I will start by showing you a screenshot of my article page on Funk Music from the Joomla! interface. Your content will look different so don't worry!

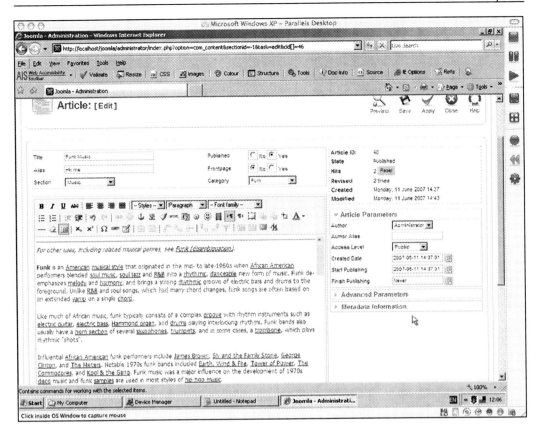

Time for Action—Adding Headings with WYSIWYG

First let's try the easier 'non-coding' or 'I don't know any HTML' way of adding headings first.

1) Say you wish to add two headings—**Complex Grooves** and **Funky Influence** to the article before the second and third paragraphs.

2) First click in the editor pane where you want to add the first heading and then type **Complex Grooves**. Then click where you want the second heading and type **Funky Influence**.

3) Now select the heading **Complex Grooves**.

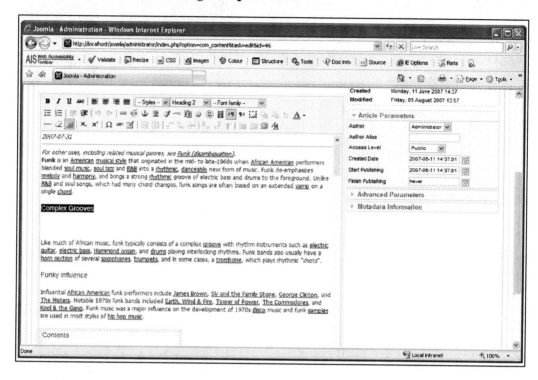

4) If you wish, make both these heading level two (<h2>). So while **Complex Grooves** is highlighted just select the appropriate heading type from the drop-down menu, **Format**, which is the second drop-down menu in the editor.

5) Follow the same procedure for the heading **Funky Influence**.

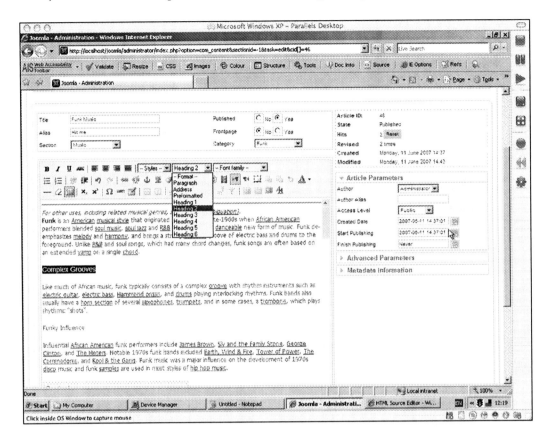

6) When you are done, click the **Save** button at the top right of the page.

7) You will then be taken to a page, which contains a list of all the content in the Joomla! database.

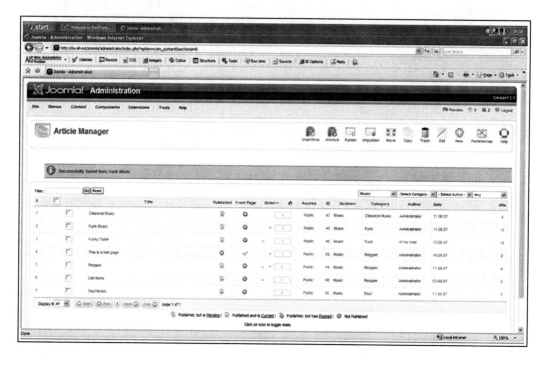

8) Click on the article you are working on. In this case it's **Funk Music**.

9) To see what the page looks like, click on **Preview**. The following page should be observed:

What Just Happened?

It may not seem like it, but by adding appropriate headings to your site content, you have taken a big step towards creating a more accessible website. This is because selecting a heading and using **Heading 2** from the **Format** menu adds the necessary HTML needed to structure your content, which basically, in each instance looks like as follows:

```
<h2>Complex Grooves </h2>
<h2>Funky Influence </h2>
```

Why do you need to do this? Sighted users can look at a page and quickly see if there are bold, large headings in a different color, and where each section of the page's content begins and ends. The sighted users can also quickly assess what parts of the page are of interest to them by reading those headings. They can then skip and read the sections of interest. Now let's have a look at achieving the same effect. But this time, we'll roll our sleeves up and edit the HTML ourselves.

You don't really have to know any code to use the editor, but I do recommend that you try and learn the basic principles of HTML coding as it will make it easier for you to understand and make changes if necessary, to make your pages more accessible.

Joomla! has limitations when creating accessible content and there is really no substitute for getting your hands dirty, if you feel confident to do so, and making adjustments to the code when necessary.

Time for Action—Adding Headings by Editing the HTML

Sometimes it's useful to edit the HTML directly. Let's see how we would go about doing the same thing by editing the HTML.

1) Click on the **HTML** button in the editor and view the source code. The following screenshot will give you an idea of what the source code looks like.

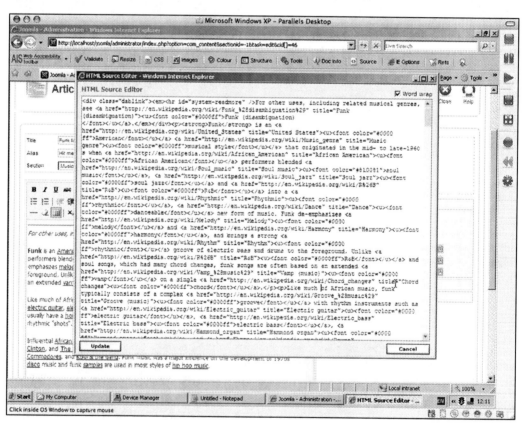

What the editor will display is not for the faint hearted as it is very hard to distinguish one piece of code from another.

You may find it useful to use another editor for writing HTML that makes is easier for you to format and read your code. Once you have written it you can paste the code directly into Joomla!.

There are lots of free (or very cheap) HTML editors available, even Notepad can be used to write your HTML. One such good, free, and accessible editor is PSPad.

You can get it at: www.pspad.com/

If you feel confident enough you can enter the HTML directly into where you would like it to appear within the site content. Remember that the bits in pointy brackets are instructions for the user agent. Focus on the normal 'English' and you should be able to find the right place.

 Adding line breaks to your code makes it easier to read and manage.

Say you wish to add two headings—**Complex Grooves** and **Funky Influence** to the article before the second and third paragraphs.

2) Add the heading **Complex Grooves** to the appropriate place in the editor and wrap the text in <h2> and </h2> tags. So it looks as follows:

```
<h2>Complex Grooves </h2>
```

3) Follow the same with **Funky Influence**, so it looks as follows:

```
<h2>Funky Influence </h2>
```

Add Frequent Headings to Assist the Screen Reader

Screen reader users often browse a web page by its headings—that is a difficult concept to explain if you have never seen a screen reader being used.

This is how it works.

The screen reader will use a particular keystroke combination; for JAWS (*Insert + F6* or the *H* key or the number keys) or for Window-Eyes (the number keys and *H*), and then a dialogue window will open, which will contain all the marked up headings (if you do it).

The screen reader user can then choose the heading that sounds like their topic of interest by using the arrow keys to move up and down through the list and when they hear something that they like, focus on that section of the page by pressing Return/Spacebar.

Why is this useful? It's useful because a sighted user can quickly scan a long or complex document and easily view the sections that are of interest to them. This visual scanning acts as a navigation mechanism allowing the user to jump over unrelated or uninteresting content. Blind users cannot do this and must use their screen reader and—if there are no structured headings—go through, line after line of content until they hit something of interest. This can be very annoying and tedious especially if the document is very long. So when using Joomla! make sure that you have structured your content correctly. It's not important that the headings should be strictly in the right 'semantic order' (though it's advisable). What is more important is that they should be there in the first place—as they are vital for accessible navigation.

Remember that screen readers are *linear output devices* (for more see Chapter 3), which means they output items on a page one at a time, so if there is a lot of content on your page, applying headings gives the page a structure that allows the user to easily navigate, without having to read loads of content that is of no use, value, or interest to them.

How to Use Different Levels of Headings

HTML headings have six levels of importance. The following table is an example of how these headings may be applied to an online article about "Travel around North America".

Heading 1 <h1>	Travel around North America
Heading 2 <h2>	**(East Coast) Things to see in North America**
Heading 3 <h3>	Places to stay on the East Coast
Heading 4 <h4>	Best restaurants on the East Coast
Heading 5 <h5>	Getting around the East Coast
Heading 6 <h6>	If you hire a car
Heading 2 <h2>	**(West Coast) Things to see in North America**
Heading 3 <h3>	Places to stay on the West Coast
Heading 4 <h4>	Best restaurants in the West Coast
Heading 5 <h5>	Getting around the West Coast
Heading 6 <h6>	If you hire a car

Heading 2 <h2>	**(Southern States)Things to see in North America**
Heading 3 <h3>	Places to stay in the Southern states
Heading 4 <h4>	Best restaurants in the Southern states
Heading 5 <h5>	Getting around the Southern states
Heading 6 <h6>	If you hire a car

You may have seen headings called 'Styles' in Microsoft Word. They are very important as they add structure to your documents. In fact, they should be called 'Structure and Styles'. Giving your Word document a suitable structure also means that you can save it in other formats and the structure will be maintained. This is really very useful indeed!

The following table gives an example of the most appropriate way of using headings in most content articles:

Heading 1 <h1>	You will use this only once per page, to provide a title for the article or main content.
Heading 2 <h2>	Use this to break the article up into suitable major sections.
Heading 3 <h3>	Use this to pinpoint particular areas in the article, and assist flow within sections.
Lower-level headings (<h4>, <h5>, <h6>)	Use in long articles if you want to build an even deeper 'hierarchy'.

All other headings can be used as needed. For example, if you have a very long article with detailed sub headings that are buried deep down within it—you might have to use <h4>, <h5>, or <h6>.

When the sub headings are used up and you have to start a new section you can start with your <h2> headings. For example, a detailed article on "Travel around North America" may have the structure as shown in the first table. I have outlined the headings and not the content. Note that I have made the higher level <h2> headings bold to show how the higher level headings can be used again after finishing a section of content.

You don't bounce from <h3> to <h6> within a section as headings are to be used to let the user know about level of importance and should follow a logical order within a document.

The fact that when you apply a `<h1>` heading makes some content look big in your browser, or small with a `<h6>`, is immaterial (the appearance of the HTML headings can be styled anyway using CSS).

What is important, is the idea is that the user, in this case of an assistive technology, can infer a sense of importance from the value the author gives to each heading.

There are ongoing debates about various subtleties of exactly how this should be done, but for some basic rules:

- There should only be one `<h1>` (Think of Highlander).
- The rest of the headings can be used as often, as needed.
- Headings should ideally follow a logical order.

In truth I would not get too uptight about the page structure being absolutely correct all the time. In my experience most AT users will be glad that the headings exist and will not quibble about how you do it. Having said that, though, it's always nice to do things properly.

Another Important Element

The following outlines what "lists" are in HTML. We will also look at how to mark up list items and when to use them.

Lists

Using lists items is also important when appropriate.

As with just making headings look big, it is not enough to just use an * or a - to signify list items. There is specific HTML code that you need to use in order to mark up lists. Fortunately the Joomla! WYSIWYG makes it simple to create lists.

Time for Action—Adding Lists

The following screenshot has a simple list of **Motown Artists.** Say you wish to turn it into a list. The text **Motown Artists** is made `<h2>` using the **Format** drop-down menu.

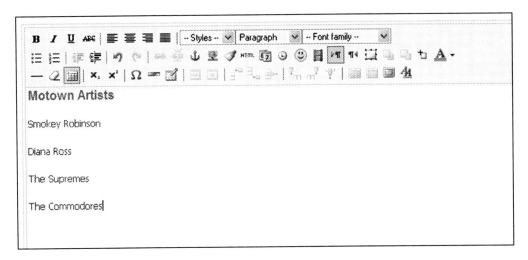

2)Highlight the list items that you want to turn into a list and then press the **Unordered list** button in the WYSIWYG toolbar.

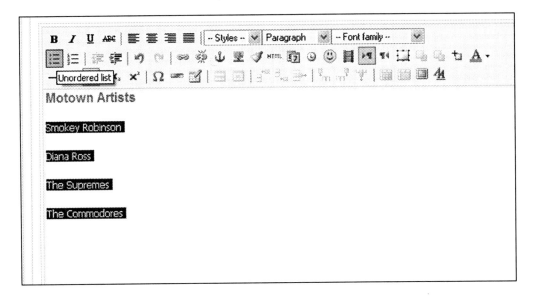

3) The items will then be displayed as a properly marked up bulleted list as shown in the following screenshot:

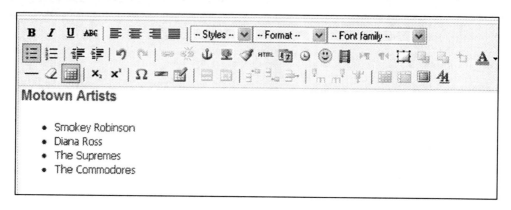

What Just Happened?

Grouping related items not just looks good visually, but also helps the non-sighted users. When a screen reader comes across a list—whether it is an ordered or unordered list—it will be announced to the user that there is a group of list items. The user can then use the arrow keys to cursor up and down between the various items in the list.

Here is the HTML for an unordered list.

```
<ul>
<li>My first list item </li>
<li>My second list item </li>
<li>My third list item </li>
<li>My fourth list item </li>
</ul>
```

Here is the HTML for an ordered (numbered) list using the <ol> element.

```
<ol>
<li>My first list item </li>
<li>My second list item </li>
<li>My third list item </li>
<li>My fourth list item </li>
</ol>
```

Website navigation links can also be marked up as list items; after all they are nothing but a group of related links.

Make Images Accessible

Web content makes extensive use of images. Sites that don't have some graphical content can tend to bore a lot of readers. In order to be truly accessible you need to describe the contents of images to non-sighted users.

We do this by providing Alt text for images ("Alt" here is short for "alternate"—a textual description of the image if the user is browsing with images off or if they are non-sighted users).

Description Anxiety

Alternative description of graphics is very much a moot point in the accessibility circles and the debate runs along the lines of what should or should not be described and how this should be done.

A textual description of the image should be considered as an equivalent form of access to the informative or descriptive content of the image. Essentially it is a subjective assessment (you make up your own mind as to what is good or what is not—what seems appropriate for one use case may not be for another). So it can be tricky for someone new to accessibility to figure out what they should or should not be describing.

So I wish to make the process a little easier for you. You may hear someone say that efforts should be made to describe every image that the web page contains that has some informative value. This might not always be the case at all.

For example if the body text of an article contains similar information to that contained in the graphic, then there certainly would be no need to describe the graphic again. Consider how your users will access this information and view all the content on your page. The screen reader user may not appreciate having the same information given twice.

Time for Action—Adding Alternate Text to an Image

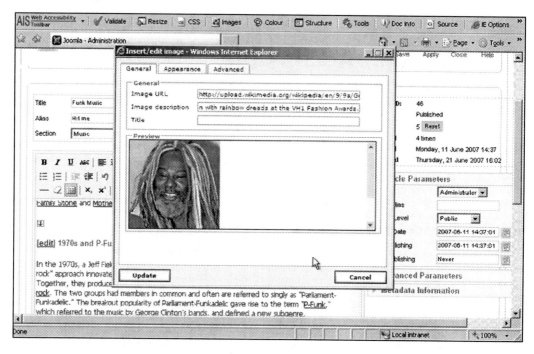

Click on the **Insert/edit image** tab to first insert the image—browse to your site directory where the image is contained.

Under **General** in the **Image description** field add your alt text to the image.

By adding your description of the image to the **Image Description** field you will effectively add your alt text to the image.

What Just Happened?

Above, two methods of providing an alternative description of an image are described. This will be useful for screen reader users and allow them to get a sense of what the contents of the image are.

The second method is also useful, say in an academic environment where a great deal of descriptive information is often needed that goes beyond a mere brief alternate description.

Both the `alt` and the `longdesc` attributes are very useful for blind users who need them in order to describe the contents of an image. When the screen reader comes across an `alt` attribute with some content, it will start reading it out straight away when the image has focus.

When the `longdesc` attribute is discovered the screen reader (say JAWS) will announce something like 'Graphic' (announcing to the user that there is a graphic present) followed by the alt text, which you added to say "Maggot Brain cover of lady with Afro screaming." If you have added a `longdesc` attribute, "Press enter for long description" then by pressing 'Enter' the HTML page that contains the long description will open in a new browser window (if the user is on IE7 it will be a new tab) and then they will treat the page like they will any other and read the contents.

Choosing Good Alternate Text for Images

Writing good alternate text is a quality issue. Here we will examine what makes good alternate text and when to use it and when not.

What is Good Alternate Text?

Images fall into two general categories — Presentational and Informative. Presentational images can be thought of as images that enhance the look and feel of your website, and are therefore used for aesthetic purposes. Other images may be informative — contain information that is of some use to the viewer to aid their comprehension of a topic or to illustrate some point.

You may ask why. Pointlessly describing images of no real informative value can be very annoying to blind users. Choosing good alt text depends on what the purpose of the image is. Generally, images can be:

- Purely decorative.
- Charts, graphs, and infographics — where an image is used to convey information. Generally, you may want to just sum these up for the reader.
- Photographs. These can be decorative or informative, depending on the context. Your choice of suitable alt text will depend on this.

Let's look at each of these in turn.

Ignoring Purely Decorative Images

If the image is purely decorative, and has no informative value etc. then give a null value to the image. Giving a null value means adding `alt=""` to the image element, with no space in the brackets. So the code for a purely presentational image could look something as follows:

```
<img src="arrow_icon.png" alt="" />
```

 This is actually very easy to do using Joomla! As whenever you insert an image using the WYSIWYG editor `alt=""` is added by default. This means that screen readers will effectively ignore the image.

Charts, Graphs, and Infographics

If an image is a graph of statistical information, a histogram, or similar, a good idea is to describe the thrust of what the graph says as your alternate description. For example, if a graph shows the amount of money people spend on their pensions, and you have several classes grouped by periods of 5 years.

The graph could look as follows:

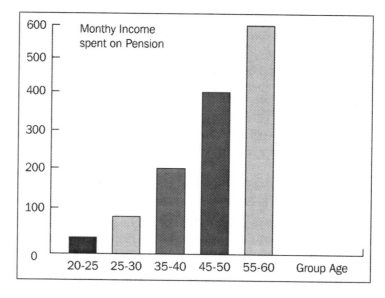

There are two approaches. You could get into the nitty-gritty of the graph by describing that the class spend in the age group 20-25 was €25 per month, the class spend in the age group 35-40 was €200 per month, etc. in your text description. However, with more complex graphs, it can be very time consuming. However, there may be times when this would be the best approach. Alternatively you could just describe the thrust of what the graph is trying to illustrate by saying: "People in their twenties spend a much lower percentage of their income on pensions, and as the sample population gets older, the amount of income spend increased dramatically".

There is an art to writing good alt text and it's a skill that, with practice, can be acquired over time.

Describing Photographs

Even within a news article, photographs can be used as a decorative element, or as a key part of the story. Whether or not you add alt text to photographs will depend on the part that the photograph plays in your content and how important you feel describing that content is to a non-visual user or a user who browses with the images off.

If a pretty photo of the mountains of Mourne, with blue skies, high flying birds and the Irish Sea is in a web page, the blind user may wish to have that image described, but on the other hand, depending on context, they might not.

You may be asking yourself should I say things like "Here is a picture of my cat" or "This is my house". By and large these kinds of descriptions are pretty useless. Instead of merely stating what something is you should take time to describe it.

If there was a picture of your cat you could say something like: "Here is my Himalayan longhaired cat. He has longer than average grey hair with lighter grey and slightly orange colored streaks running through it. He has bright intelligent green eyes".

Do you see the difference?

Time for action—Using longdesc

Another way for more detailed descriptions, is to use a `longdesc` attribute. This allows you to add more descriptive text to your images by pointing to another page that contains the more detailed description of the image.

1) Firstly write a new HTML page that contains the text that you wish to use as your description. This page should only contain information that is related to the `longdesc` and not any other content. You can use HTML headings to structure the page if needed and mark up paragraphs using the `<p>` element.

It may be better (easier) to create a separate HTML file in another editor like PSPad or Notepad that contains the longdesc information and bring this HTML file into your site directory.

2) Save the file in a suitable directory—maybe the same one that contains the HTML file you are viewing. When you have done this save the file and give it a name that is intuitive and relates to the content. So if the longdesc is about describing one of Henry the Eight's wives say Catherine Howard, call the file catherine.html or howard.html. If the longdesc content is about your favorite Funkadelic album, call it maggotbrain.html etc. Do you get the idea?

3) You will be able to see the **longdesc** field by clicking on the **Advanced** tab in you images options.

4) Add the address of the page that contains the longdesc.

There may be situations where this would be useful—for images that really do need a long suitable description that could be many paragraphs long, however in many cases it probably won't be needed.

However, if there are situations where you feel your image content needs a more detailed description then it will be useful.

What Just Happened?

Longdesc is really useful in an academic setting where a great deal of descriptive information is often needed that goes beyond a brief alternate description.

When the longdesc attribute is discovered by the screen reader it will output something like 'Graphic' (announcing to the blind user that there is a graphic present) followed by the alt text which you added earlier say "Maggot Brain album cover of lady with Afro screaming" then (if you have added a longdesc attribute it will immediately output "Press enter for long description". Then when the user presses *Enter* the HTML page which contains the long description will open in a new browser window (if the user is on IE7 it will be a new tab), and then they will treat the page like they will any other and navigate or read the contents in the normal manner.

 "A picture is worth a thousand words" goes the old saying. So now you can see what it is like when the shoe is on the wrong foot and you are trying to figure out what the thousands words are that describe the picture!

Good Link Text Assists Accessibility

You can make your site much more accessible by using descriptive link text. Doing this (when you think about it) makes a lot of sense but it is certainly not always applied in the wild.

Avoid links that use the text 'click here', as you could have several links on the page which say 'click here' and a blind user is therefore not informed what the link is for, where it will bring them, or what they can expect when they get there.

Include text that describes what the link is for and where it goes in your links. Screen reader users will thank you for it and find your site much more pleasant to use. Graphic designers may not like this as it makes link text longer but you can compromise.

As mentioned previously when we were talking about headings, a screen reader user can extract the headings from a page and browse the site by selecting the sections of interest to them. They can do exactly the same with links. By extracting the links from the page the screen reader user can see exactly what the links of interest are and where they go. This is why taking time to name your links in a descriptive manner is really useful and goes a long way towards building real accessible websites. You don't have to go overboard with your link text, but try and think about how a blind user would access your content.

The following example will give you a clear idea.

Joshue O Connor's accessibility verdict	Sample link text	Reason
Bad	Click here	The link text contains no information at all about what will happen when I "click here".
Better	Click here for more information	The link text now tells me to expect "more information"… but what about?
Best	More information about funk music	I know that the link provides more information about funk music. And the uncomfortable suggestion that I must be using a mouse (and clicking on a location) has been removed.

Creating Accessible Tables

Tables got a bad review in accessibility circles, because they used to create complex visual layouts. This was due to the limitations in the support for presentational specifications like CSS and using tables for layout was a hack—that worked in the real world—when you wanted to position something in a precise part of the web page. However, this was not a good idea for all users, and we will find out why and what to do about it in Chapter 5.

Tables were designed to present data of all shapes and sizes, and that is really what they should be used for.

The Trouble with Tables

So what are tables like for screen reader users? Tables often contain a lot of information, so sighted users need to look at the information at the top of the table (the header info), and sometimes the first column in each row to associate each data cell.

Obviously this works for sighted users, but in order to make the tables accessible to a screen reader user we need to find a way of associating the data in each cell with its correct header so the screen reader can inform the user which header relates to each data cell.

Screen reader users can navigate between data cells easily using the cursor keys. We will see how to make tables accessible in simple steps.

There are methods of conveying the meaning and purpose of a table to the screen reader user by using the `caption` element and the `summary` attribute of the table element that you will find more on in the next section.

We will learn how to build a simple table using Joomla! and the features contained within the WYSIWYG editors that can make the table more accessible. Before we do that though I want you to ask yourself about why you want to use tables (though sometimes it is unavoidable) and what forms should they take.

Simple guidelines for tables:

1. Try to make the table as simple as possible.

2. If possible don't span multiple cells etc. The simpler the table, the easier it is to make accessible.

3. Try to include the data you want to present in the body text of your site.

Time for Action—Create an Accessible Table (Part 1)

In the following example we will build a simple table that will list the names of some artists, some albums they have recorded, and the year in which they recorded the albums.

1. First of all click the table icon from the TinyMCE interface and add a table with a suitable number of columns and rows.

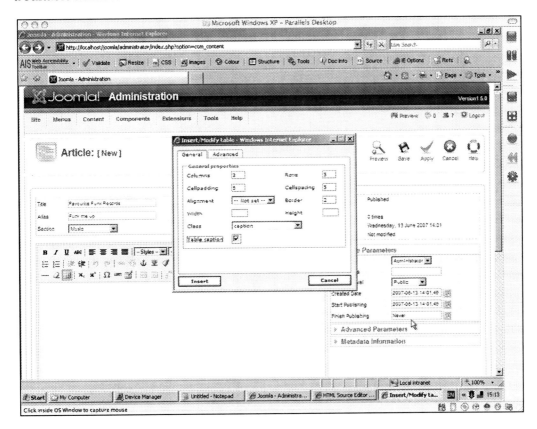

2. By clicking on the **Advanced** tab you will see the **Summary** field. The summary information is very important. It provides the screen reader user a summary of the table.

For example, I filled in the following text: "A list of some funk artists, my favorite among their records, and the year they recorded it in".

My table then looked as follows:

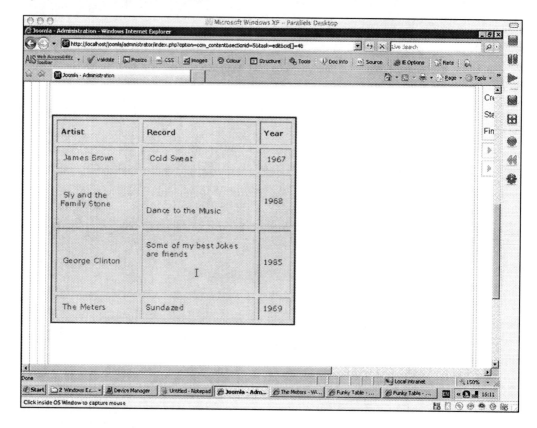

What Just Happened?

There is still some work to be done in order to make the content more accessible. The controls that the WYSIWYG editor offers are also a little limited so we will have to edit the HTML by hand.

Adding the summary information is a very good start. The text that I entered "A list of some funk artists, my favorite among their records, and the year they recorded it in." will be read out by the screen reader as soon as it receives a focus by the user.

Time for Action—Create an Accessible Table (Part 2)

Next we are going to add a Caption to the table, which will be helpful to both sighted and non-sighted users. This is how it's done.

Firstly, select the top row of the table, as these items are the table heading. Then click on the **Table Row properties** icon beside the **Tables** icon and select **Table Head** under **General Properties**. Make sure that the **Update current Row** is selected in the dialogue box in the bottom left. You will apply these properties to your selected row.

If you wish to add a caption to your table you need to add an extra row to the table and then select the contents of that row and add the Caption in the row properties dialogue box. This will tell the browser to display the caption text, in this case **Funky Table Caption**, else it will remain hidden.

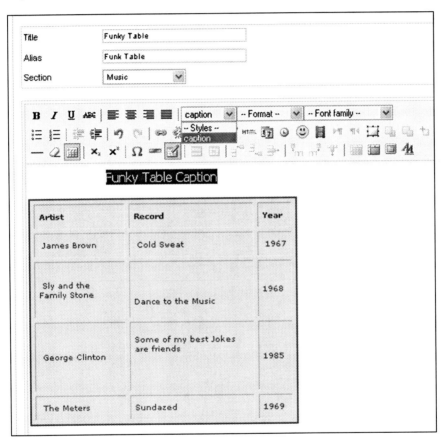

What Just Happened?

By adding caption to the table, you provide useful information to the screen reader user. This caption should be informative and should describe something useful about the table. As the `caption` element is wrapped in a heading it is read out by the screen reader when the user starts exploring the table—so it is slightly different to the `summary` attribute, which is read out automatically.

Does it Work?

What we just did using the WYSIWYG editor, TinyMCE, is enough to make a good start towards creating a more accessible table, but we will have to work a little more in order to truly make the table accessible. So we will now edit the HTML.

The good news is that you have made some good steps in the right direction and the final step is of associating the data cells with their suitable headers, as this is something that we cannot really do with the WYSIWYG editor alone, and is essential to make your tables truly accessible.

Time for Action—Create an Accessible Table (Part 3)

By selecting the table and pressing the **HTML** button in the editor you should see the following table code:

```
<table border="2" cellspacing="5" cellpadding="5" width="350"
   summary="a list of some funk artists my favorite of their
   records and the year they recorded them in.
   " style="width: 350px; height: 288px; background-color: #f8e906;
   border: #361fdf 2px solid" dir="ltr" id="PFunk Table"
   lang="English">
<thead>
  <tr>
    <td>
      <strong>
        Artist
      </strong>
    </td>
      <td>
        <strong>
          Record
        </strong>
      </td>
      <td>
        <strong>
          Year
        </strong>
      </td>
  </tr>
</thead>
<caption class="caption">Funky Table</caption>
<tbody>
  <tr>
    <td>
      James Brown
    </td>
```

```
        <td>
          Cold Sweat
        </td>
          <td>
            1967
          </td>
    </tr>
<tr>
  <td>
    Sly and the Family Stone
  </td>
      <td>
        <p>
          Dance to the Music
        </p>
      </td>
        <td>
          1968
        </td>
</tr>
<tr>
  <td>
    George Clinton
  </td>
      <td>
        <p>
          Some of my best Jokes are friends
        </p>
          <p>
             
          </p>
      </td>
        <td>
          <p>
            1985
          </p>
        </td>
</tr>
<tr>
  <td>
    The Meters
  </td>
      <td>
        Sundazed
      </td>
        <td>
            1969
        </td>
</tr>
</tbody>
</table>
```

Now we will add the `header` and `id` association. This is a way of associating the contents of a data cell with its appropriate header, so that when a screen reader user navigates to a cell, the screen reader will announce what column the data cell is in.

This is how you make `header` and `id` association—first you deal with the headers and the table body:

Give each header a unique id; in this example the `id` is same as the contents. For header 1 id="Artist", header 2 id="Record" and header 3 id="Year".

In HTML code this will look as follows:

```
<th id="Artist">Artist</th>
<th id="Record">Record</th>
<th id="Year">Year</th>
```

It could just as easily be:

```
<th id="header1">Artist</th>
<th id="header2">Record</th>
<th id="header3">Year</th>
```

Or any other suitable naming convention that makes sense for your tables. Now that we have established the header and ids, we need to associate them with the cell contents of each row in the table body as follows.

```
<tr><td headers = "Artist">James Brown</td>
<td headers = "Record">Cold Sweat</td>
<td headers = "Year">1967</td>
</tr>
```

That takes care of the first row, now for the second and subsequent rows:

```
<tr>
<td headers = "Artist"> Sly and the Family Stone</td>
<td headers = "Record">Dance to the Music</td>
<td headers = "Year">1968 </td>
</tr>
<tr>
<td headers = "Artist">George Clinton</td>
<td headers = "Record">Some of my best Jokes are friends </td>
<td headers = "Year">1985</td></tr>
<tr>
<td headers = "Artist">The Meters</td>
<td headers = "Record">Sundazed</td>
<td headers = "Year"> >1969 </td></tr>
</table>
```

Putting it All Together

So by looking at what we have done, can you see how the associations between headers and each data cell have been made? Look closely and you will see that it makes sense.

```
<th id="Artist">Artist</th>
<th id="Record">Record</th>
<th id="Year">Year</th>
<tr><td headers = "Artist">James Brown</td>
<td headers = "Record">Cold Sweat</td>
<td headers = "Year">1967</td>
</tr>
<tr>
<td headers = "Artist"> Sly and the Family Stone</td>
<td headers = "Record">Dance to the Music</td>
<td headers = "Year">1968 </td>
</tr>
<tr>
<td headers = "Artist">George Clinton</td>
<td headers = "Record">Some of my best Jokes are friends </td>
<td headers = "Year">1985</td></tr>
<tr>
<td headers = "Artist">The Meters</td>
<td headers = "Record">Sundazed</td>
<td headers = "Year">1969 </td></tr>
</table>
```

So now you know what the correct accessible HTML should like. Now let's look at the code as it will appear in your WYSIWYG editor with the summary attribute, the caption element, etc.

```
<table border="2" cellspacing="5" cellpadding="5" width="350"
summary="a list of some funk artists my favorite of their records
and the year they recorded them in. " style="width: 350px; height:
288px; background-color: #f8e906; border: #361fdf 2px solid" dir="ltr"
id="PFunk Table" lang="English">
<thead>
<th id="Artist">Artist</th>
<th id="Record">Record</th>
<th id="Year">Year</th>
</thead>
<caption class="caption">Funky Table</caption>
<tbody>
<tr>
<td headers = "Artist">James Brown</td>
```

```
<td headers = "Record"> Cold Sweat</td>
<td headers = "Year">1967</td>
</tr>
<tr>
<td headers = "Artist"> Sly and the Family Stone</td>
<td headers = "Record">Dance to the Music</td>
<td headers = "Year">1968 </td>
</tr>
<tr>
<td headers = "Artist">George Clinton</td>
<td headers = "Record">Some of my best Jokes are friends </td>
<td headers = "Year">1985</td></tr>
<tr>
<td headers = "Artist">The Meters</td>
<td headers = "Record">Sundazed</td>
<td headers = "Year">1969 </td></tr>
</tbody>
</table>
```

What Just Happened?

The first two steps were a lot like creating any table, but we then took some extra steps with the HTML to make sure the table was really accessible.

- We added a summary that can be used to summarize the contents of the table for the blind user. The contents of the summary attribute are not displayed visually in the browser. This summary information is really useful to a screen reader user when they first navigate to a table. It is read out automatically if present and the blind user can therefore get a quick and clear overview of the purpose of the table and its contents.

- We added a caption so that the both the visual user and the screen reader user can get a brief overview of the purpose of the table. The caption element is displayed visually and read out by the screen reader when the user starts to explore the table.

- Tweak the headers by editing the HTML as shown. This, as you now know, helps to make the association explicit and makes the table truly accessible.

By following this advice tables can be useful for both sighted and non-sighted users.

Does Joomla! Have Good Table Manners?

I found the capabilities of creating accessible tables limited. When I tested with a screen reader I could navigate around the table, but could not easily figure out what piece of cellular data was associated with what header.

However, after tweaking the HTML, the table turned out just fine.

I believe that the new version of TinyMCE (2.0) has the capability of adding the `scope` attribute to the table editor to make more complex tables accessible. An accessible table marked up using the `scope` attribute would look something like this:

```
<!DOCTYPE HTML PUBLIC "-//W3C//DTD HTML 4.01 //EN"
"http://www.w3.org/TR/html4/strict.dtd">
<html>
<head>
<meta http-equiv="Content-Type" content="text/html; charset=utf-8">
<title>Tables with scope</title>
</head>
<body>
<TABLE border="1"
        summary="This table charts the number of cups
                of coffee consumed by each senator, the type
                of coffee (decaf or regular), and whether
                taken with sugar.">
<CAPTION>Cups of coffee consumed by each senator</CAPTION>
<TR>
    <TH scope="col">Name</TH>
    <TH scope="col">Cups</TH>
    <TH scope="col" abbr="Type">Type of Coffee</TH>
    <TH scope="col">Sugar?</TH>
<TR>
    <TD>T. Sexton</TD>
    <TD>10</TD>
    <TD>Espresso</TD>
    <TD>No</TD>
<TR>
    <TD>J. Dinnen</TD>
    <TD>5</TD>
    <TD>Decaf</TD>
    <TD>Yes</TD>
</TABLE>
</body>
</html>
```

While the `scope` attribute is well supported by most screen readers available nowadays; the support was somewhat limited in the older screen readers (< JAWS 6, though it was technically supported since version 4.5 it was very patchy). So using the combination of `headers` and `id` may be better if you wish to support the older screen readers, but in general using `scope` attribute is also fine for marking up tables. How you mark up your tables depends on the content and how you wish to present it. A good rule of thumb is the simpler the better.

Summary

In this chapter we have learned how to:

Use headings and other HTML elements to provide content structure. Doing this will make your website more accessible to people with disabilities who use assistive technology, as well as those on mobile devices. Also there are SEO (Search Engine Optimization) benefits to structuring your content as search engines often look for keywords or pattern match sets of keywords and then return those results to the user.

Provide simple text alternatives to images and use the `longdesc` attribute for more detailed descriptions. While you may not use the `longdesc` attribute in your projects, it is still very useful to many blind users when they need detailed information about a diagram or image. Use descriptive link text to assist accessibility. We learned how a simple and common sense approach to your link names can be very beneficial to many users. Create tables and how to make them more accessible by editing the HTML by hand.

5
Creating Accessible Templates

If you're not familiar with creating Joomla! templates, you can read Packt Publishing's *Joomla! Template Design*, by Tessa Blakely Silver. This chapter assumes that you already know the basics of Joomla! templates, and will focus on ensuring that your templates designs are accessible, and outline what to look out for when you design templates to ensure that they look smart and can be used by everyone.

Understanding How Joomla! Templates Work

Designing Joomla! templates certainly requires a different approach to the usual web standards-based site design. It needs a little bit of lateral thinking and good planning to get it right from the very beginning. The more time and effort you put into thinking about your design needs, the modules that you need to use, the better it pays off in the end. So getting it right with Joomla! really does mean, good planning.

Earlier versions of Joomla! (<1.5) also used tables for layout. This goes against the grain of accessible web standards design. While it is not always a showstopper, it is not an ideal development method as it is preferential to use various CSS `<div>` elements as containers for your Joomla! module content. This is possible with Joomla! 1.5, so let's look at this issue first.

 I use the term web standards to refer to best practice in web design and development. For more on web standards have a look at the following website www.webstandards.org.

Separation Anxiety—Layout Tables, HTML, and CSS

A big step forward in recent years has been the move towards separating the code that is used to mark up content (HTML) from the code that you use to tell the browser for displaying that content (CSS), and also from code that tells the content how to behave (JavaScript).

While using Joomla! you won't really have to worry about this as Joomla! manages your HTML, CSS and JavaScript files, but in principle it's important to note some of the benefits. They are as follows:

- Site content is easier to edit and maintain. HTML files are not cluttered with `<font>` tags and style information, and as a result, are much lighter and easier to understand.

- Good housekeeping. If you need to edit how something looks you will need to use the CSS file. If you wish to change a behavior, you edit the JavaScript file. This again makes managing your projects much easier. Revisiting a site for a client, to make some changes in what you built over a year ago could be a nightmare if all the elements were mixed up haphazardly.

- Clean HTML generally lends itself to more structured content, which means more accessible websites. And more accessible websites are also more SEO friendly, as search engines like Google, etc. often look for keywords in the headings.

Joomla! 1.0 Used Tables for Layout, So What's the Problem?

As we saw in the last chapter, tables were originally designed to work with tabular data. They were not designed to be used as mere scaffolding for images at all, which is what they often became when used online. As William Gibson said, "The street finds its own uses for things".

In the last decade most of the sites that you must have seen used tables for layout (and many still do) including earlier versions of Joomla!. This was due in part to limitations in the support for presentational specifications like CSS, and using tables for layout was basically a hack, or fix—that worked in the real world—when you wanted to position something in a precise part of the web page—such as a company logo or other graphics.

Unfortunately, designers were forced to resort to such ingenious methods to make their websites work. This was because you could not rely on how the various browsers would present your styled content. This lead to all sorts of complex hacks and multiple versioning and other time consuming methods, poor designer had to come up with to get the pages to look the same in multiple browsers.

Why Are Tables Bad for Layout?

Firstly when tables are being used as placements for images and general layout duties, they are not being used for what they were originally designed for. Many web standards people will rightly say that this reason is enough for not using them, especially as the graphical web no longer needs tables to hold it all together, as browser support for CSS has improved greatly.

Secondly, when you use tables for layout, it means a lot of tables on your page. Tables within tables (nested tables) and so on. This can get messy — but for whom? Well apart from the coder having a hard time coming up with ever more ingenious ways to use tables to support their designs, blind users using screen reader software can have a hard time when a website has a lot of tables.

Why? Since there is just no indication for a screen reader user about the purpose of the table, and as the table element was designed for presenting tabular data, there are no specific attributes to support their use for layout. So the tables that are invisible to the sighted person, who just sees a nice website layout. Whereas the screen reader user often has to listen to the screen reader output 'table', 'table',..'table' for each table that is included in the site. This can impact negatively on the usability of the site and the quality of the browsing experience for a screen reader user.

As I mentioned there are no support attributes that make it easier for screen reader users, when tables are used for layout. There is however another 'hack'. It is to use the `summary` attribute of the `table` element. The `summary` attribute can be set to say `<table summary="This table is used for layout">`, but this will not be ideal if there are 20 tables outputting this information; it can be tedious for a screen reader user to listen to.

In real terms, tables for layout can be more annoying to a screen reader user than a cause of any major accessibility problems. So it really is a usability issue rather than an accessibility issue. This is because content can often be buried under a lot of tables, and using lots of tables combined with insufficient semantic structure can spell a really hard time for users of assistive technology.

Having said that though, who wants to annoy their users!

We are not going to look at the older methods of using tables for layout, as was the way for many of the older Joomla! templates, and instead we will concentrate on using a more web standards-based approach.

Building a Standards-Compliant Joomla! Template from Scratch

As I mentioned earlier I am assuming that you already know how to build a Joomla! template. What we will focus on here is what to look out for, whilst ensuring that the template is as accessible as possible. Once you have got to grip with how to build your template, or modify an existing one, for it to be considered more accessible, there are only a couple of major issues that you need to keep in mind while designing. There are many advanced aspects of using Joomla! templates, such as using image replacement techniques for graphical headers, or adding AJAX functionality; and these have specific workarounds in order for them to be considered accessible. However, there are more advanced techniques that we will not cover here as what I want is for you to start with an accessible canvas that you can later add to, if you wish.

So briefly I will look over what core areas you need to have ready in order to put the whole thing together and then I will build a template theme based on Funk Music called the "Funk Factory".

 All of these areas (and some more advanced techniques) are covered in greater detail in Tessa Blakely Silver's very useful *Joomla! Template Design* book.

What Modules Do I Need?

You should have a clear idea of all the modules that you wish to include in this project and the functionality that each of them has. Each module function is loaded with the following code.

```
<jdoc:include type="modules" name="user1" style="" />
```

`<jdoc:include type="module"` refers to the module that you wish to insert in your webpage, `name="user1"` is the module position (you set what modules go into what position in the **Module Manager).**

The function also has various `style` options that take the following arguments `0,1,-1,-2,-3` that allow the following options when it comes to developing your template.

The `style` option `-2` allows you to wrap modules in a single `<div>` element and section titles in `<h3>` tags.

The `style` option `-3` will wrap modules in a several `<div>` elements and titles in `<h3>` tags.

These will be the probable settings you will be using. You may also want menus to be displayed as 'flat lists' and these headings are available in the Joomla! Administration panel, within the **Module Manager** by choosing **Flat List** from the **Menu Style** option.

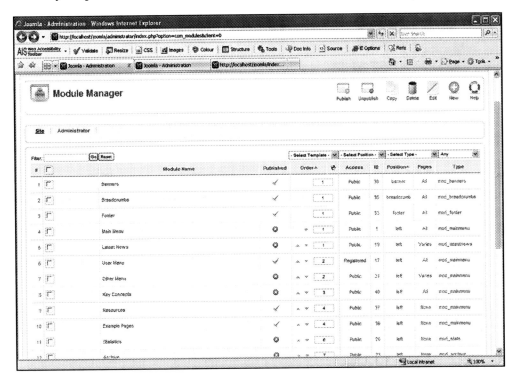

Joomla! arranges everything in your website by using **Module Positions**. These are Left, Top, and Right and can be considered to be like scaffolding for your content, which is going to come from **Site modules.** **Site Modules** are like the building blocks of your site and contain your content.

You can position multiple **Site Module** content by stacking them in a module position such as to the left, right or top of your page and determine the order they appear in by giving each module a number. So a site module with an order value of **1** will appear first, **2** will appear second, and so on.

Color scheme

It really is worthwhile spending time to come with a suitable color scheme for your Joomla! site. This can be difficult if you have no experience of design but don't fear. It's not as difficult as you think. Here is my color palette for my 'Funk Factory' template. I haven't decided what I will use each color for at this stage, but I will completely base my choices on my chosen palette.

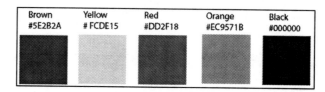

Some useful things that you can do to find ideas for your color palette are as follows:

- Look at websites that have color schemes that you like and ask yourself: "What is it about these colors that works well together?". Don't be shy about using color schemes you see on other sites, on your own site. The Web is a highly derivative medium, which is a posh was of saying "everyone copies everybody else". Just make sure you take inspiration from the best!

- Take inspiration from art, nature, posters you see, and magazines that you read.

- Understand your audience. Who will be using the site? Is it for a young hip crowd? A more corporate look or a community website? All these factors will influence your decision and should inform the color choices that you make.

Ensure Good Color Contrast for Your Site

Try and ensure that there is sufficient color contrast used on your site, especially when displaying text such as headings and other content. There are tools available to measure whether the color contrast works and if there could be problems for visually impaired people. These include Gez Lemon's excellent 'Luminosity Contrast Ratio Algorithm' (`http://juicystudio.com/article/luminositycontrastratioalgorithm.php`), which was later added to Steve Faulkner's AIS Accessibility Toolbar (`http://www.webaim.org/articles/ais/`).

These tools are really useful to check if the color contrast is sufficient or not. It is rather difficult to make this judgment correctly yourself, especially if you are not familiar with the needs of users with limited or residual vision combined with the effect that various retinal conditions can have on a person's visual perception. Low vision users are some of the users that will benefit the most from your accessible template design. Choosing a good color scheme is a rather simple, but very effective, way of creating a more accessible website.

However, a certain degree of common sense will help you figure out if there would be any problems. For example, using a light blue text on a dark blue background, or a light green text on a light green background will not help, and I hope that you can easily grasp why!

You can also offer the user a choice of different style sheets if the user requires a higher contrast version. You could use large yellow text on a black background and that would really help users with limited vision.

Icons and Graphics

Create all the graphics that you want for the project before you go to Joomla!.

 If there are certain graphics that a client wishes you to use, like a logo or photographs of certain products, etc. — then you may also get ideas for a suitable color scheme from them. Just remember how important good contrast is!

When using icons to indicate certain sections or functionalities of your site, decide on a look and feel and then design suitable logos that fit your needs. How they look will depend on many of the issues that you saw in the last section on colors and audience.

 If you are not good with graphics there are websites such as MaxPower where you can find quality free icons to use in your projects (http://www.maxpower.ca/).

Create a Mock Up If Possible

If you can, design a full mock up of the site template in your favorite image editor. This will allow you to play with different ideas and give you something tangible to reach for when you start coding. Don't worry if the final version of your site doesn't exactly match your mock up, and on the other hand your final site might be better than what you thought it would!

Following is a screenshot of some graphics that I did in Adobe Illustrator for my template 'Funk Factory'. The design will be tweaked later and I have included placeholders to indicate roughly where I hope to include the final Site Module content.

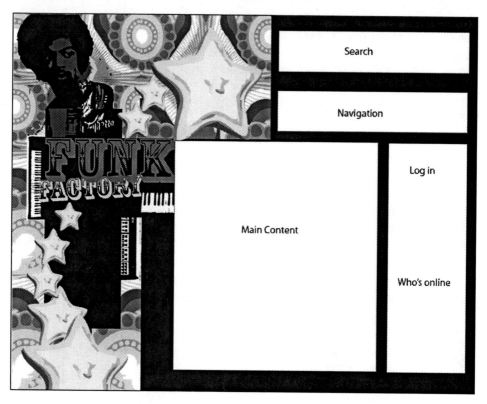

Roll Your Own Accessible Joomla! Template

As I mentioned you will pretty much have to create your own template from scratch when you want to build a nice accessible standards-compliant website. Don't be put off by this task. If you are familiar with CSS and have some web design experience, the extra steps and lateral thinking needed to style your site using Joomla! are really in the planning and preparation stages where you figure out the modules, colors and graphics that you want to use.

Using Dreamweaver

If you are using Dreamweaver there are a couple of things that you can do to make developing the template easier. The first thing is to download the excellent (and free) extension developed by Daniel Duvald. It can plug into Dreamweaver, where you will see it as an option at the top of your workspace menu which contains the options **Common**, **Layout**, **Forms**, etc., and lets you edit your templates much more quickly.

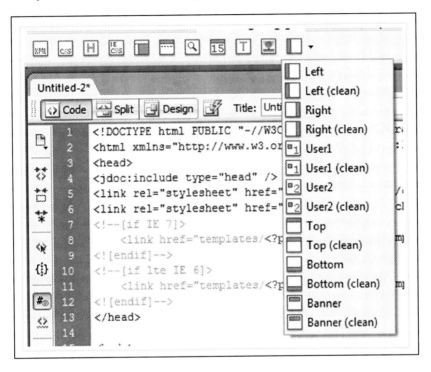

You can use this extension to edit your PHP file, add XML data, and insert various pieces of module code for Joomla! 1.5.

Set Up FTP Server Connection to Your Local Host

Set up an FTP connection to your local host in your WYSIWYG editor such as Dreamweaver. You may be used to doing this for websites that are hosted remotely. The process is exactly the same except that here, you point to a directory on your own machine.

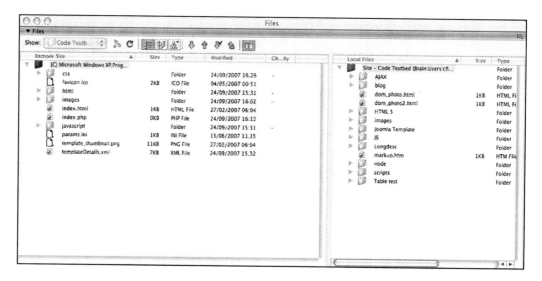

You can then make changes to your code, and save directly to the host server (which is the quickest way), or copy your files to your host server after you make changes, refresh your browser and see the changes you have made. This will be your basic workflow.

 You will also need to run a local server application such as Xampp where you will install Joomla!. I like Xampp as it is easy to install and use. For more on setting up and using a local server, consult the following website: (http://www.apachefriends.org/en/xampp.html)

Create a Template for Your Template

For the creation of my 'Funk Factory' template, I took an existing template (Beez) and made a copy of it in my htdocs/templates folder of my local host server. I then renamed the entire folder Music and this folder then became my basic Joomla! universe (meaning all the files that I need for my new template will be contained here). I could then manage the new template from my administration section of my Joomla! installation. From here I could edit HTML and CSS if I wish, though in this case I am happy to use Dreamweaver for the editing tasks and then upload the files to my local host server.

A Few More Steps, Before We Get Going with Coding Our New Template

1. Open the `index.php` file on your local host server. If you are using Xampp, it will be in the Templates folder, which is a sub folder of htdocs. All these files are in the xampp folder, which will be wherever you installed it on your C drive if using a PC or another suitable directory.

2. Select the contents of the file and delete them.

3. Don't worry about what you just did. Joomla! will populate the file with the necessary information needed to make your website work.

4. Open all the CSS files and do the same. For this example I will try to use only one CSS file, though in principle having several that contain different layout details can be a good idea and makes the content easier to manage. If we need more than one, later we can add our CSS declarations to more than one file.

5. Open the templateDetails.xml file and edit the text between the <name></name> tags to reflect what you are calling your template. In this case I called it Music so the code now looks as follows:

```xml
<?xml version="1.0" encoding="iso-8859-1"?>
<install version="1.5" type="template">
  <name>Music</name>
  <version>1.0.0</version>
```

Selecting Your Template

Once you perform the above steps, you can select your new template and apply it as your default in the Joomla! administration panel. To do this you must:

Go to **Extensions -> Templates Manager**.

Select the template you have named by clicking on the radio button beside the name. In this case I called mine **Music**.

Select the **Default** button (the large yellow star).

This will make your new template the Joomla! default one.

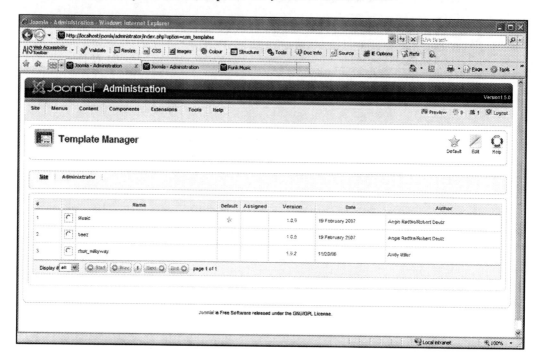

Choosing the Correct DOCTYPE

The first thing that we are going to do is add a DOCTYPE to our template (the
`index.php` file). This will then be applied to every page throughout the site. The
subject of DOCTYPES is probably not one that you will need or wish to give much
attention to, but it is important to understand what they represent and why they are
important.

The DOCTYPE basically determines the HTML or XHTML version that your Joomla!
site will use. The two main DOCTYPES that we will be concerned with are the
`Strict` and `Transitional` DOCTYPES.

The `Strict` DOCTYPE is rather like its name implies; a form that means that your
pages must conform, or be syntactically correct, or the web pages will be at best,
considered invalid or at worst, not rendered at all.

The `Strict` DOCTYPE looks like this:

```
<!DOCTYPE html
PUBLIC "-//W3C//DTD XHTML 1.0 Strict//EN"
"http://www.w3.org/TR/xhtml1/DTD/xhtml1-strict.dtd">
```

The `Transitional` DOCTYPE is more forgiving and while you must use the syntax of XHTML if you have regular HTML elements and attributes, or presentational elements, jumbled up in your code you will still be able to produce a conforming web page, which is a another way of saying you can get away with more when you code! You can also use this DOCTYPE for browsers that don't do CSS.

The `Transitional` DOCTYPE looks like the following:

```
<!DOCTYPE html
PUBLIC "-//W3C//DTD XHTML 1.0 Transitional//EN"
"http://www.w3.org/TR/xhtml1/DTD/xhtml1-transitional.dtd">
```

So we will use a `Transitional` DOCTYPE for our template. In order to support some older Joomla! modules that use tables or contain presentational elements in the code they output, you may also need to stick with the `Transitional` DOCTYPE as using the `Strict` DOCTYPE could break them, or render them invalid.

What's up DOC?

What are the advantages of using various DOCTYPES? Well, earlier in the book I had mentioned that we will mostly use HTML in our code (as I didn't want to scare you!). I will use XHTML with the `Transitional` DOCTYPE for the rest of the book. To make this leap is really no big deal.

In many ways HTML 4.0 is absolutely fine for even the most cutting edge of web development. XHTML is a serialization of XML, which is another way of saying; XHTML is an XML like language, while HTML has its roots in the older SGML. XHTML is an extensible-markup language. This means that it can be expanded with many useful bespoke features. You can't do the same with HTML.

XHTML Rules

XHTML code must be written in lower case (all elements and attributes),

All elements must be closed, even empty elements (so you write <br />)

Attribute values must be quoted and may not contain any blank spaces. Get into the habit of use an underscore "_" to separate attribute values or even longer file names.

Elements must be nested properly. For example:

```
<p><strong>this is wrong</p></strong>
<p><strong>This is right</strong></p>
```

So I hope that you can see that using XHTML is not such a great leap. In fact, with time you will understand that it all comes down to good authoring practice, and helps to keep your code tidy and easier to manage.

Just One More Thing

I am also going to add a couple of more pieces of code just to go that extra mile. Firstly, they declare the language of the document we are using, which is English and secondly, to tell the browser what kind of content it can expect to come across within the document that its going to render (i.e. your web pages):

```
<html xmlns="http://www.w3.org/1999/xhtml" xml:lang="en" lang="en">
<meta http-equiv="Content-Type" content="text/html; charset=UTF-8" />
```

Both of these pieces of code can go directly after your DTD or DOCTYPE declaration.

Putting It All Together

Add the transitional DOCTYPE to your `index.php` file along with the other code I have shown. Your `index.php` page should look as follows.

Add the following XHTML code after the DOCTYPE and save the file:

```
<html>
<head>
<title>Funk Factory Template</title>
</head>
<body>This is where your body contents go.</body>
</html>
```

Enter the URL to the local host where your `index.php` file is located. It should look something the following:

```
http://localhost/joomla/index.php
```

Refresh your browser and you should see something like the following screenshot:

 If you got the previous screenshot, well done! Though it may not be very exciting yet, you are on your way! If not please make sure that you have either uploaded the index.php to the local host server or saved the index.php file properly.

Basic Template Layout

In order to get the ball rolling with the layout we will start with a more traditional page layout, which I drew in Adobe Illustrator, and then further style it to fix the template's design requirements. A basic template layout for my requirements will look something like the following screenshot. Please note I have indicated what kind of module or functionally I would like each part of the page to contain. The design may also change and I have not decided if I want the module content to span the entire page or to be placed within a moveable <div> container element. The best thing about working like this is that you can tweak your design as you go. At this stage it is important to have an idea of the functionality that you want your site to have, and roughly what you want it to look like.

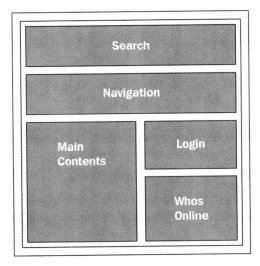

I then create the container <div> elements within my index.php file, which are going to act as containers for each of the site modules I have illustrated. The code for the <div> elements for each section looks like as follows:

```
<body>
<div id="main_wrapper"><!--Main wrapper for all content -->
<div id="search">
Search Feature goes here
</div><!--//Search-->
<div id="navigation">
Navigation Menu goes here
</div><!--//Navigation-->
<!-- Start wrapper for main content, login feature and whos online -->
<div id="content_wrapper"> <!--Secondary wrapper for main content etc
-->
<div id="main_content">
Main Content will go here
</div> <!-- //main_ content-->
<div id="login">
Login feature and who is online
</div><!--//login feature -->
<div id="whoisonline">
Login feature and who is online
</div><!--//who is online -->
</div> <!-- //main_wrapper-->
</body>
```

Save the file and refresh your browser and you should see something like the following:

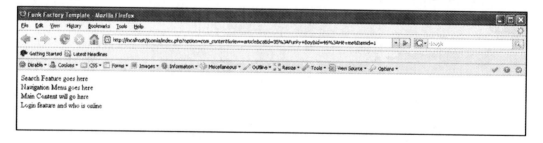

What you see in your browser is a simple textual outline where later the content will be inserted from the MySQL database that is styled using CSS and hopefully looks the part!

The next step is to write the CSS code needed to create something more along the lines of my original outline. So you can think of this stage as the scaffolding stage.

CSS Scaffolding

In order to make the CSS easier to code and manage, I am going to create two separate CSS files; one for layout and the other for finer presentational declarations. You may want to put all your CSS declarations into one file; and even that is fine. I am going to separate them as this can be an easier way of managing your CSS, as you don't have to go through a long jumble of mixed declarations to find certain rules.

The code that will link to the CSS files looks as follows:

```
<head>
<title>Funk Factory Template</title>
<jdoc:include type="head" />
<link rel="stylesheet" href="templates/<?php echo $this->template ?>/
css/layout.css" type="text/css" />
<link rel="stylesheet" href="templates/<?php echo $this->template ?>/
css/presentation.css" type="text/css" />
</head>
```

The Joomla! extension for Dreamweaver has some useful features that will help you get up and running with designing your Joomla! site. I have an **Insert header Code** option, which literally places all of the header code that you will need from the DTD, lang information, to links to your CSS files etc. You may of course have to modify it slightly to ensure that references files etc. are correctly addressed but it is a useful feature.

My CSS Layout

Here is the CSS that I need, to position everything where I need it. I have added some presentational declaration so you can see the positioning of the `<div>` containers.

```
/* CSS Document */
/* Layout of Funk Factory Template */
/*Wrappers */
  #main_wrapper   {
  margin: 60px auto;
  padding: 10px;
  padding-left: 200px;
  width: 800px;
  border: 10px solid #fff;
  }
  #content_wrapper   {
  background: #ccc;
  color: #333;
  margin: 10px auto;
  padding: 10px;
```

```
        padding-bottom:300px;
        border: 10px solid #ccc;
        width: 800px;
        }
/*Search */
#search  {
width: 100%;
height: 40 px;
border: 10px solid #ccc;
padding: 10px;
}
#navigation  {
width: 100%;
height: 40 px;
border: 10px solid #ccc;
padding: 10px;
}
/* Main Content */
#main_content {
width: 60%;
background: #fff;
margin: 10px 10px 200px 10px;
padding: 25px 20px 20px 20px;
border: 10px solid #ccc;
float: left;
}
/*Site Module Layout*/
#login {
width: 20%;
background: #fff;
margin: 10px;
padding: 25px;
float: right;
}
#whoisonline  {
width: 20%;
background: #fff;
margin: 10px;
padding: 25px;
float: right;
}
#footer  {
clear: both;
width: 100%;
height: 10 px;
border: 10px solid #ccc;
padding: 10px;
}
```

After saving the file and refreshing the browser my layout looked as follows:

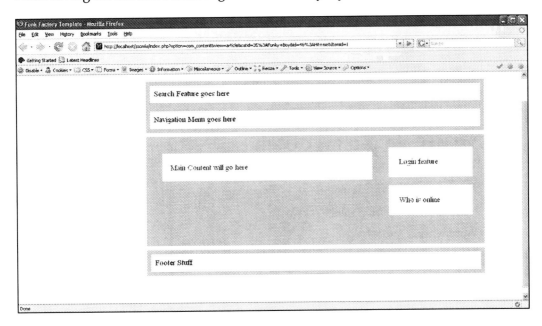

Just Before We Add Any Content Modules

Using the Joomla! extension for Dreamweaver is really useful as it makes important things like adding the links to your various CSS files, adding the title information and other metadata really easy with Joomla!. By pressing the **Insert header code** button you will get everything from the DTD to the META data from your configuration settings, all at the click of a button!

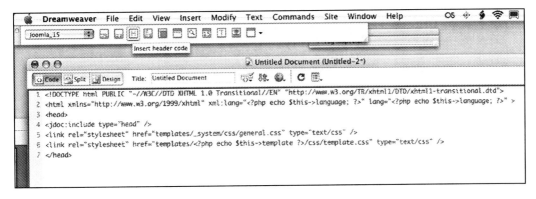

Adding Content Modules

At this stage you should know what modules you wish to use in your project. If not, go to the **Module Manager** in your Joomla! administration section and find out more about the modules that are available and what they do. For my project I wish to use the following modules:

- Search Module (mod_search)
- Top Menu (mod_mainmenu)
- Polls (mod_poll)
- Who's Online (mod_whoisonline)
- Login Form (mod_login)
- Breadcrumbs (mod_breadcrumbs)
- Footer (mod_footer)

The syntax for adding your modules to your `index.php` file is as follows:

```
<jdoc:include type="modules" name="user3" style="-2" />
```

The name of the module is `user3` and the style value of `-2` is a way for you to control how Joomla! will output the module content. So I need to add the above line of code with the name of each of my modules above into my `index.php` file. The final file will look as follows:

```
<!DOCTYPE html PUBLIC "-//W3C//DTD XHTML 1.0 Transitional//EN"
"http://www.w3.org/TR/xhtml/DTD/xhtml-transitional.dtd ">
<html xmlns="http://www.w3.org/1999/xhtml" xml:lang="en" lang="en">
<meta http-equiv="Content-Type" content="text/html; charset=UTF-8" />
<html>
<head>
<jdoc:include type="head" />
<link rel="stylesheet" href="templates/<?php echo $this->template ?>/
css/layout.css" type="text/css" />
<link rel="stylesheet" href="templates/<?php echo $this->template ?>/
css/presentation.css" type="text/css" />
</head>
<body>
<div id="main_wrapper"><!--Main wrapper for all content -->
<div id="search">
<jdoc:include type="modules" name="top" style="-2" />
</div><!--//Search-->
<div id="navigation">
<jdoc:include type="modules" name="user3" style="-2" />
```

```
</div><!--//Navigation-->
<!-- Start wrapper for main content, login feature, whoisonline and
poll -->
<div id="content_wrapper"> <!--Secondary wrapper for main content etc
-->
<div id="main_content">
<div id="pathway">
<jdoc:include type="module" name="breadcrumbs" /></div>
<jdoc:include type="component" />
</div> <!-- //main_ content-->
<div id="login">
<jdoc:include type="modules" name="right" style="-2" />
</div><!--//login, whoisonline and poll feature -->
</div> <!-- //content_wrapper-->
<div id="footer">
<jdoc:include type="modules" name="footer" style="-2" />
</div> <!-- //Footer-->
</div> <!-- //main_wrapper-->
</body>
</html>
```

Note that the code

<div id="login">

<jdoc:include type="modules" name="right" style="-2" />

</div>

Inserts the three modules (**Login, WhoisOnline** and **Poll**) neatly into
<div id ="login"> as I have set them the module position right in the
Module Manager.

On saving file and refreshing the browser the following output was obtained:

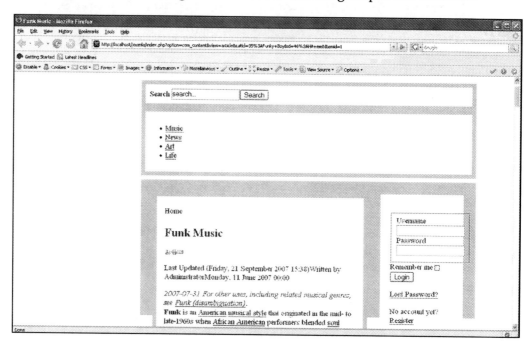

Note that the main content area of my site is not a module, but a component. This piece of code actually inserts your main site page content into your web page, so it is very important.

The tricky things about working with Joomla! is getting used to how Joomla! deals with the content. Remember that it is a CMS, therefore it needs a robust way of managing a lot of content and functionality, which can take some time getting used to. When you design your layout you really need to understand where you want things to go and create `<div>` placeholders using CSS. Then by using a combination of your **Module Manager** and a useful tool like the Joomla! Dreamweaver extension, you can populate those place holders with module content.

The hardest thing I found, when I first used Joomla!, was knowing how to reference your modules or what they are called. The funny thing with Joomla! is that you don't really call or insert a module into your container `<div>` 's by its name such as `mod_search` or `mod_mainmenu` and so on.

You actually arrange the position of the modules using the **Module Manager** and arrange them into suitable 'slots' like top, left, right, etc. These are the Module position slots that you then insert into your `<div>` elements. Say if you place three modules in the 'right' slot and then place that slot in a suitable `<div>` each of the modules will slot nicely in on top of each other.

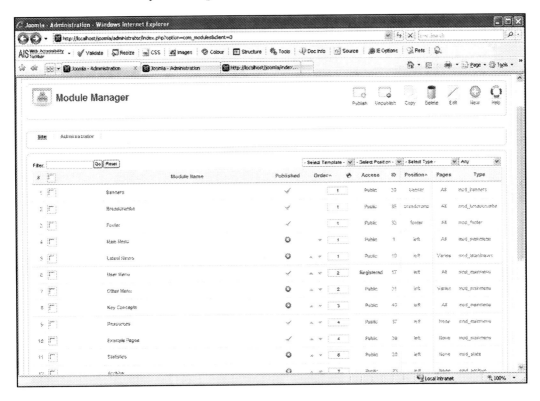

You arrange the order in which they display in the **Module manager** by clicking on a particular module and entering the **Edit Module** page. You then add your desired module to a suitable position such as top, left, right, and so on. This is the key to adding your modules to your website using Joomla!

With Joomla! you can slot several modules into one position such as left, right, top, etc. by giving the module you want to appear on top a value of '1', the next one '2' and so on. You can easily rearranging the order by changing the module's display settings.

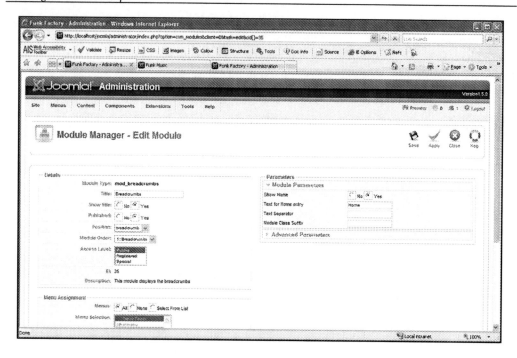

I have broken up my layout to show what slot relates to what module, so that you get a better idea. It can be confusing at first, but hang in there and persevere, as once you get used to developing like this, it opens a world of possibilities.

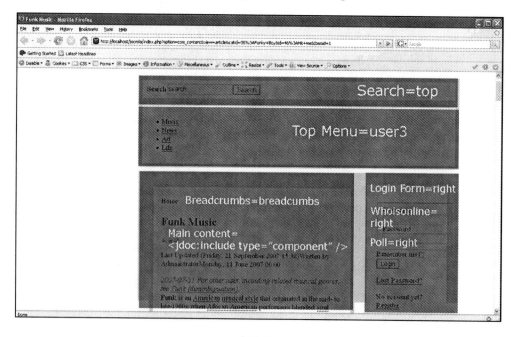

Module Options

Module options are really useful for controlling how Joomla! outputs the content. They also perform some important accessibility related functions. The style value when you add module information to your `<div>` containers:

```
<div id="login">
<jdoc:include type="modules" name="right" style="-2" />
</div>
```

`-2` in this case will mean that the modules are displayed in a `<div>` with module titles in `<h3>` elements. The style option takes several arguments `0`, `-1`, `-2`, `-3`. The first two values output the modules within tables so you will never really use them. Both `-2` and `-3` however give you room to modify how your module is presented using CSS.

Finishing the Template

Learning more about CSS is the best way to get the most out of your designs. Some great places for you to learn more are: A list apart (`http://www.alistapart.com`), CSS Beauty (`http://www.cssbeauty.com`), W3 Schools (`http://www.w3schools.com`) and CSS Zen Garden (`http://www.csszengarden.com`).

All that's left now is to finally finish off the design and in effect add a suitable skin to your projects. In order to get the most out of Joomla! I recommend that you try and get better at CSS and you will in no time be producing visually pleasing and accessible websites.

At this stage you will have done most of the hardest part of getting your project off the ground. Finishing the template is a case of styling it to suit your needs. In order to be able to style my interface I will have to look at the source code in my browser by going to **View -> Source in IE or View -> Page Source** in Firefox. There we will see the class names and ids that Joomla! generates when it inserts a module into your webpage. These then act as 'hooks that you use for your CSS declarations.

Following screenshot shows the final template:

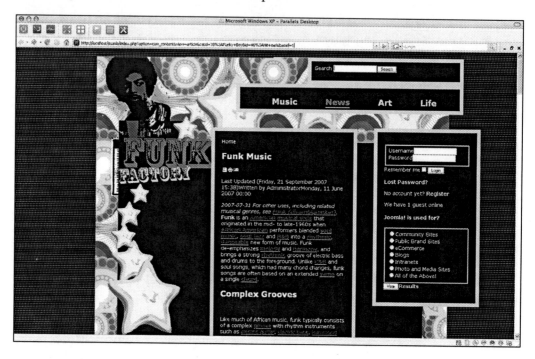

Advantages of Joomla! Templates

By using a template that is well designed (or by building your own), you will have gone a long way towards having a more accessible website before you even write a line of code or add any content.

 There are several sites that offer high quality commercial templates for Joomla! that are graphically sophisticated and have been designed to be accessible such as Yootheme (http://www.yootheme.com) and Rocket Theme (http://www.rockettheme.com/).

So what are the advantages of using Joomla! templates?

There is a complete separation of content from presentational elements. Using CSS for layout means that you are using the right tool for the right job. Leave the tables for your tabular data and nothing else.

One of the greatest benefits of CSS is that by changing a rule in the CSS declarations, you can change the entire look and feel of all of the elements of your site that use that rule.

This makes site design and maintenance so much easier than having to individually change each instance of each element like you had to do with inline styles (back in the day).

It therefore means that when you use a template for your site's design, by making simple changes to your template you can make radical changes site wide, very easily.

Easily change the site's design completely by adding a new template and 'Hey presto' you now have a complete new look for your website.

Editing Joomla! Templates

Joomla! makes it rather easy to edit existing templates or to create your own.

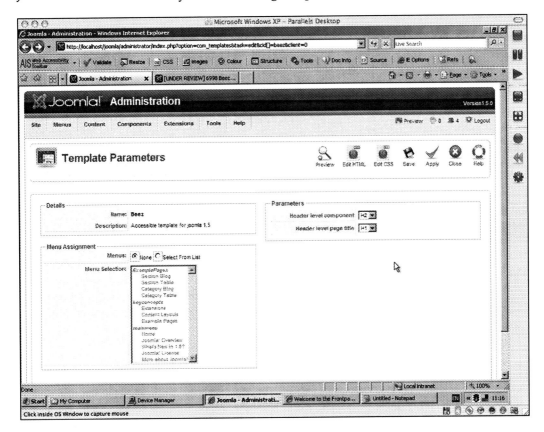

Existing template parameters can be edited to suit your needs, as can the template's HTML and CSS using Joomla!'s own edit facility if you don't use an editor.

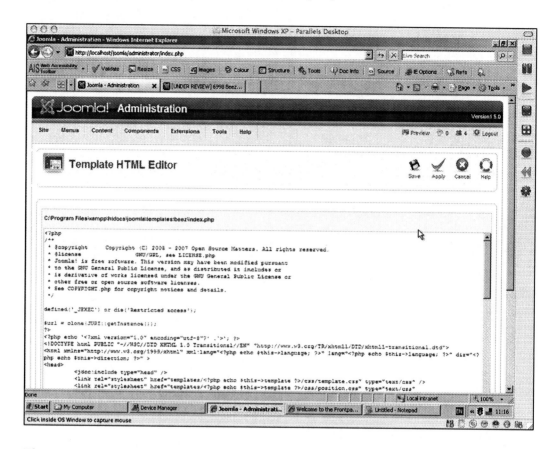

The CSS template editor is very useful as it gives you the ability to select and modify all the various style sheets that your site uses whether for printing out the pages of your site or adding certain style sheets to serve to other browsers or platforms like mobile devices, PDA's and so on.

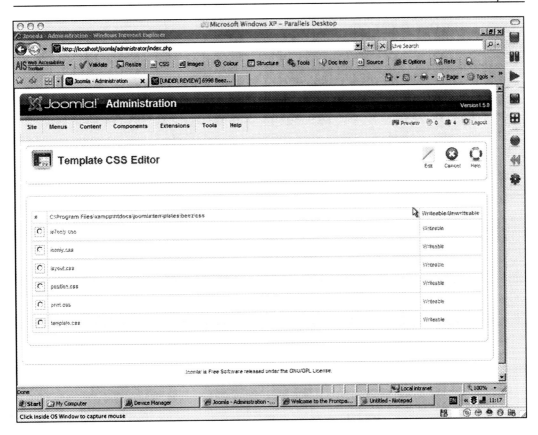

This obviously gives you a great deal of control over your site's design and layout but also means that many accessibility issues can be easily avoided by using well designed accessible templates for all of the sites that you build with Joomla!. Ensuring that you use a well designed template means that you can concentrate on structuring your content and improving the information architecture of your projects knowing that the templates that you use are already well designed, can have sufficient color contrast and are a solid foundation for all of your Joomla! projects.

We have looked at the needs of users with low vision and using a color scheme that has sufficient color contrast is a great help. But what else should you be aware of? Here are some other pointers what will help to make your site more accessible.

Resizable Text

Many users with low vision will need to be able to resize the text. All modern browsers have the facility to be able to resize the text using the browser's built in controls. Some websites have a widget, which allow the user to increase or decrease the font size by pressing a + or – sign. While these are OK to add if you wish, there are not really necessary, as many users who require large text will already know how to increase the font size using the browsers built in controls.

How to Make Sure That Text Will Resize

Always use a relative font size in you CSS. This means using % or ems. For example:

```
#Joomla_em_header h3 {
  border-top: 1px dashed #cccccc;
  border-bottom: 2px solid white;
  padding: 25em;
  background-color: #666666;
  color: #ffffff;
  font-size: 1.2em;
  }
#Joomla_percentage_header h2  {
  color: #fff;
  font-size: 110%;
  padding: 2px;
  text-align: center;
  }
```

Both % and em are relative font sizes. This means that they will display the content relative to how the page author (you) sets it. So you can make all text large by default by setting this value in your style sheet and then by giving the specific site content (various headings, paragraphs or list items) higher or lower % values. The declarations that you write will make the headings etc. appear to be larger or smaller, as you wish.

Do not use px or absolute font sizing. Using pixel values means that your font will stay that size even if the user tries to resize your text in their browser. Hence the name absolute!

Without a Mouse

When building your site make sure that users can get around the site content without a mouse. This means that your site must be keyboard navigable. Many users will prefer to use the TAB key to navigate about your page and this method of interaction is therefore very important for people who have limited physical mobility, tremors or who have had a stroke. In fact it is preferable to try any make all your sites work without your users having to use a mouse at all. I don't have a physical disability and I still like to be able to navigate a website using my keyboard.

 The TAB order of elements in Joomla! may sometimes be difficult to control as content is pulled out of a MySQL database and the way modules are presented may change from page to page in your website.

Unfortunately, there are only two elements within a webpage - when coding with HTML - that can actually receive focus when navigating by the keyboard and they are anchor elements and form control elements.

These are the elements that the user can use to TAB through the interface. The order that these anchor tags (hyperlinks), or form controls, appear within the source order of your pages code then determines their tab order when the user is navigating via the keyboard. Please be mindful of this when you build your site and adopt a common sense approach to your information architecture and how your structure your page. People with limited mobility who can get to sections of the site with a small number of clicks will thank you for it.

Highlighting Links

CSS can also be used to highlight the elements on the page that have focus at any point in time, which is really useful so the user can visually follow where the TAB order is going, as well as their place in the web page. This is useful for everybody and can have a particular use for low vision users as well as users with cognitive or intellectual disabilities as it can help to aid comprehension and orientation.

I will show you some sample code that you can use in your Joomla! projects to highlight the link that has focus. It's not complex at all and can be easily added to your CSS style sheet.

Some Basic Link Styles

The following is a basic link style that will make your link red. Note that you can of course use any color of hex value that you need.

```
a  {
color: red;
}
```

This can be added to for various effects such as underlining your link text.

```
a  {
color: red;
text-decoration: underline;
}
```

If you don't wish to underline your link text you can add the declaration `text-decoration: none;` or leave it out altogether.

```
a  {
color: red;
text-decoration: none;
}
```

Now that we have a basic style what we need to do is tell the browser how and when to display the link in the way we want. This is called adding focus and is done using CSS pseudo-classes.

```
a  {
color: red;
}
a:hover, a:focus, a:active  {
color: yellow;
text-decoration: none;
}
```

Internet Explorer doesn't support `a:focus` but Firefox and other standards compliant browsers do. So this pseudo-class is there for them while IE just ignores it and actives the focus declaration when it comes across `a:active`.

So we are nearly there. There may however be a case where you will want to also change the background color of the highlighted element. This can be easily done by slightly modifying your CSS as follows.

```
a  {
color: red;
}
a:hover, a:focus, a:active  {
```

```
    color: yellow;
    text-decoration: none;
    }

    a:focus, a:active  {
    background-color: blue;
    text-decoration: none;
    }
```

There are more tweaks and improvements that you can do and I recommend Mike Cherims' tutorial on Accessites.org for more (`http://accessites.org/ site/2007/05/keyboard-friendly-link-focus/`).

Skip Navigation

Allowing users to skip over groups of links like navigation bars or other groups of content is also really useful. The Accessible Template Beez, has some nice features that do just that—for more, see the section on accessible templates.

'Skip navigation' or 'Jump to Content' links are rather easy to implement even if you don't use that template and are useful as they reduce the physical load on the user when they navigate your site via the keyboard.

It is basically a link to another link within your page, and that's it. It may look something like this:

```
    <!-- somewhere at the top of your page -->
    <a href="#content">Jump to Content</a>
    <!-- navigation links -->
    <a name="content"></a>
    <!-- start of your content or any part of page you want the user to
    get to -->
```

If you are writing in XHTML then you may wish to use both name and id attributes to ensure it works. This would look something like this:

```
    <!-- somewhere at the top of your page -->
    <a href="#content">Jump to Content</a>
    <!-- navigation links -->
    <a id="content" name="content"></a>
    <!-- start of your content or any part of page you want the user to
    get to -->
```

It may be better to say 'Jump to content' rather that 'Skip navigation'. This is because many users will not know what navigation is (seafaring analogies aside like 'surfing the web' etc). So 'Jump to content' is good, clean, descriptive and unambiguous.

Some developers also choose to hide the 'Jump' link using CSS but it may be best to leave it visible, users with cognitive disabilities may find it useful, as the page focus will shift if the page has a lot of content and jump the user right to where they want to be.

'Back to the top' links are also very useful, especially for pages with a lot of content. This principle is exactly the same.

Accessible Templates

Beez is an extended template that has been designed for use with Joomla!. This means that it is a basic template system that does some extra stuff that you may find useful. With Beez, particular attention has been paid to Web standards and accessibility.

How has this been done? Firstly, by separating the content from the presentation and layout - the benefits of this we mentioned earlier.

Secondly, Beez uses the aforementioned skip to content links, which the Beez developers call 'Jump links'. These 'Jump links' can be tabbed through by using the keyboard and brings up several options that the user can select, depending on what part of the page the user would like to get to. On the Beez website they use three categories 'Skip to Content', 'Jump to Main Navigation' and 'Jump to additional Information'. These could be useful to screen reader users who are, in a sense, given a menu that outlines the main content types on the page. The designers of Beez see this feature as being useful for screen reader users who could use the 'Jump links' to easily get to a form within the page.

'Jump links' is an optional feature in the Beez template but I think it could also be useful for users with limited physical mobility who can toggle through these options and easily select the section of the site they want. It's a nicely designed feature of the Beez template so I'll give it the thumbs up.

Beez also boasts a 'semi-scalable' layout, which means that the developers designed the template to resize. The text does resize quite well - depending on the amount of content you put on each page and where you put it. Its important that you keep your web page designs fluid and ensure that your text size can resize so visually impaired users can increase the size of the text and modify the layout size as they need to. Graphic designers love small text, as it does look cool, but it's often rather impractical. So care must be taken to be aware and your users will often really appreciate it if they can resize the text and actually read your content comfortably. Care has also been taken in this template to use relative font sizes (em) that allow your text to be easily resized.

Beez contains a font-size widget that your site visitors can use to increase or decrease the font size of your pages. There are different opinions about the efficacy of these kind of widgets - as there are already tools within the browser that can be used to resize text - so you should use your own judgment as to whether you should use them or not.

For more on Beez visit `http://www.joomla-beez.com/`.

Summary

So what did we learn?

The importance of preparation, when designing your template. As with any design project a lot of really good preparation pays off in the end. A pen and paper for mock layouts and a good idea of what you want the site to do will really go a long way to produce a high quality website.

The advantages of using accessible templates, such as being able to make quick site wide changes in your CSS and easily add new styled template to your projects.

The importance of good color contrast and making your text resizable for visually impaired users. Good color contrast improves the legibility of your content for everyone. If the site looks great and has lots of great content but is in a tiny font that no one can read then it's not much use!

How to give your links a visual focus when navigating by the keyboard. This can help users who are visually impaired as well as people with cognitive disabilities. How to 'Skip Navigation' or 'Jump to Contents' links to your pages and why they are useful to screen reader users, as well as people with limited mobility as they allow the user to easily bypass large navigation areas and other content.

6
Using XStandard to Create Accessible Content

Joomla! gives you the option of using either of the two most popular WYSIWYG editors—Tiny MCE and XStandard. For sighted users, both provide an intuitive and easy-to-use interface and both are suitable for creating accessible websites. So what you use depends largely on your own personal preference.

For a screen reader user, both the editors have improved their accessibility. In our tests, Tiny MCE was usable by a screen reader and all the various controls could be identified. However, screen reader users may also prefer to mark up their own content in a separate editor and then copy-paste the HTML code directly into Joomla! This is viable if a screen reader user finds the WYSIWYG difficult to use.

Choosing Your Editor

You can choose the editor you wish to use by going to **Global Configuration** and making your choice with the **Default WYSIWYG editor** option there.

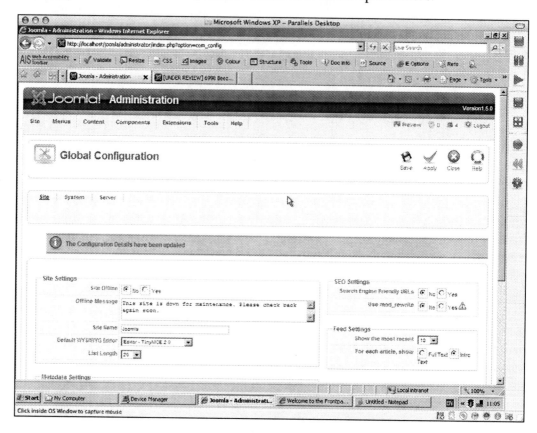

While writing this book I had some problems getting XStandard to display (due more to the fresh betas of Joomla! that I used), so I stuck to TinyMCE for most of the book and used it for many of examples in Chapter 4. I found TinyMCE effective as well (it's also quite accessible for screen reader users), but XStandard is also an excellent editor and we will cover its features in this chapter.

At the end of the day, the editor that you use really depends on your personal choice and preference.

 The latest version of XStandard 2.0 has some good accessibility features that can really help you when building your sites. It includes tools to help you generate accessible mark up, as well as a keyboard accessible interface.

The XStandard Interface

The XStandard toolbar is divided into four areas: the **Styles Menu**, **Tool buttons**, **View modes** and **Help**.

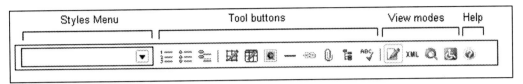

Styles Menu

The **Styles Menu** is used to format the content in the editor. First select the content in the editor pane and then the style.

For consistency of presentation, styles available in the **Style Menu** can be preset to offer formatting choices suitable to the document being edited. This would be great if your organization has a particular visual theme or style that you need to stick to when making your website.

- For speed, a single style can apply sophisticated formatting combinations, as well as structural metadata like heading information.

- For added convenience, styles can also be grouped under headings.

- When a style is selected, it displays a check mark in the drop-down menu.

Tool buttons

Tool buttons include action items, for applying bullet points, uploading a file, inserting a table, or inserting third-party content.

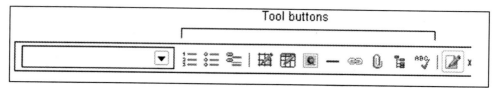

For faster access, other formatting options (such as bold and italic buttons) can be placed on the toolbar.

View modes

 In the Edit mode, if the toolbar buttons are active, it means that you, the author, can edit the content.

XML In the View Source mode the editor displays a code view of the editor's output and is intended for technical users who know how to write XHTML and wish to enter mark up directly. If mark up entered through **View Source** is not standards-compliant, the editor will attempt to correct it, or allow the user to fix the mark up manually.

Numeric values do not take quotation marks while string values do. But, when using the map notation, quotation marks are not required for property names if they are written in camel-cased DOM notation.

Please note that XStandard is designed to produce, valid XHTML 1.1 Strict. This means the editor is designed to produce only strict (or proper) XHTML 1.1. HTML lets you get away with sloppy codes, but with a little practice you will be able to know what to look out for when using XHTML 1.1.

Don't worry as the XStandard editor takes care of most of this for you but there will be times when you need to make changes to your code by hand and a good reference is useful.

Try Vlad Alexanders' really useful XHTML reference site: `http://xhtml.com/en/xhtml/reference/`.

Browser Preview

The **Browser Preview** button shows how a web browser displays content managed through the editor. Authors cannot edit content in this mode.

Screen Reader Preview

Screen Reader Preview displays content as a screen reader would process it. This will be discussed in detail later in the chapter.

Help

When available, the editor's **Help** menu links to the online version of the guide.

Context Menu

The context menu is fully accessible using a keyboard and is the quickest means for accessing all the features of the editor.

The options in the context menu are grouped by the type of functionality and may differ according to the context.

To display the context menu, right-click inside the editor, or use the following keyboard shortcuts:

Windows: *SHIFT + F10*

OS X: *CONTROL + SPACE*

Use the up/down and right/left arrow keys on your keyboard to navigate the context menu, and use the *ENTER* key or *SPACE* to select context menu options.

Removing The "Noise" From Markup

In order to help you create a good clean markup, XStandard removes what is referred to as 'noise' from your markup. This 'noise' is basically anything that should not be in a clean, standards-compliant web page. This includes deprecated tags (which are tags that were once in the specifications for previous versions of HTML, but have now been dropped, so they are technically 'illegal' if we wish to be dramatic about it).

It also uses a CSS powered **Styles Menu**.

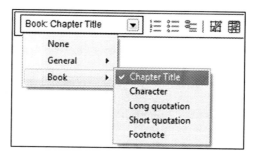

Using Correct Markup

XStandard encourages the correct use of markup by (for example) not using the `<blockquote>` element to force a paragraph indent for purely presentational purposes; so in real terms this means the editor will not display a left indent for content within `<blockquote>` elements.

`<blockquote>` should be used only for its intended purpose — which is marking up quotations.

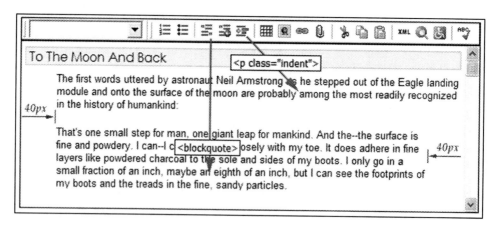

Relative Values

XStandard supports the use of relative values for text size such as % and em. Using relative units means that your users can then easily resize your site text.

 Being able to resize text is great for everyone who prefers their text to be a bit larger, such as people with vision impairments, older people, and me!

The text can be resized by using the browser's built in controls or controls that you embed in your accessible templates. If you don't want to make your own, that's fine as the browser already has the power to resize the text very well.

Decorative Versus Non-decorative Images

As mentioned in Chapter 4, it is important to know which images should be given alternate text, what appropriate alternate text is, and equally when not to use alternate text at all. XStandard makes it easy to handle either situation.

XStandard will prompt you to identify an image as Decorative or non-decorative. The editor then goes on to the **Alternate text** for all non-decorative images and also permits the author to enter a **Description** and a **Long description URL** for a more detailed description if required.

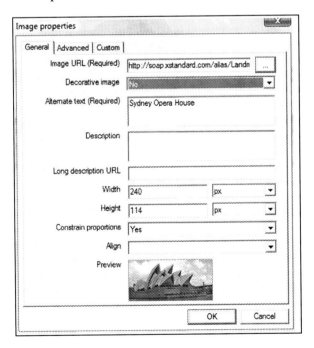

Using the **Long description URL** to provide a more detailed description of an image is useful when you are using images that really need complex and detailed descriptions. This may be the case if you work in an academic environment or something similar.

However, in some situations it may be better to include the information that the image contains somewhere in the body text if possible.

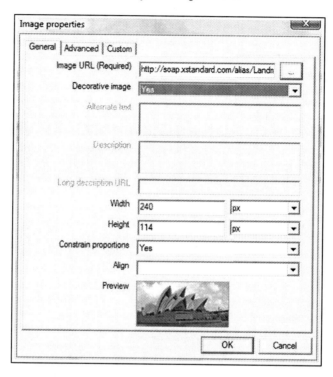

 If the image is identified as decorative, the fields **Alternate text,** **Description,** and **Long Description URL** fields are grayed out and the controls disabled.

Data Tables

In Chapter 4, we saw how to create accessible tables using TinyMCE; now we will look at using XStandard.

Although you can use layout tables in XStandard, I am not going to recommend that you do so; we will stick with using them only for data.

As we know, data tables are made up of cells that usually contain text or numbers, whose content is understood by referring the column and row headers.

As we also know, if screen readers are not made aware of the presence of column and row headers, they will process information in a data table as if it were in a layout table—reading from left-to-right, top-to-bottom. This is mostly with large and more complex tables.

For example, a screen reader that is unaware of the column headers in the table above will generate the following meaningless output:

Popular Summer availability Winter availability Greece Yes. Visitors are particularly drawn to sites of antiquity such as the Acropolis. Yes No Egypt Yes, an increasingly popular tourist spot, with pyramids being of special interest. Yes Yes

To avoid this type of confusion, XStandard requires the author to identify when a data table is being used, and ensure that screen readers are able to detect the presence of column and row headers in the table.

The following screenshot shows the results as seen in the Screen Reader Preview of the same data table. The presence of column headers has been clearly flagged by the editor, and the screen reader can now use the headers to make sense of information found in the table:

Country Greece Popular Yes. Visitors are particularly drawn to sites of antiquity such as the Acropolis. Summer Availability Yes Winter Availability No...and so on.

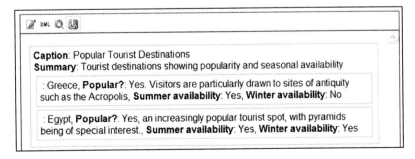

Create a Table

To create a table the following steps should be performed:

1. On the toolbar, select the **Draw data table** button ⊞. Alternatively, in the context menu, select **Toolbar -> Buttons -> Draw data table**.

2. Draw the desired number of rows and columns for the table.

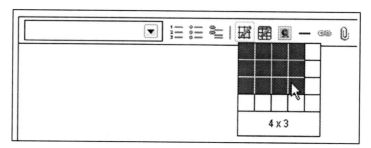

Once the table has been drawn, the **Table properties** dialog box is displayed and all the important accessibility information must be entered before creating the data table.

Edit Tables Using the Table Properties Dialog Box

The following screenshot shows the data **Table properties** dialog box. In addition to fields found in the **layout table properties** dialog box, data tables include the fields for **Summary** and **Caption**, similar to what we saw in Chapter 4.

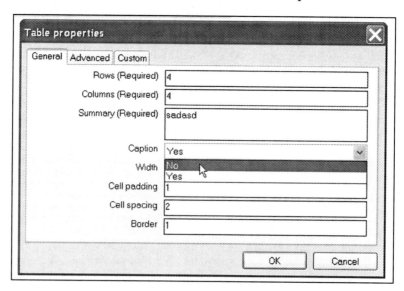

Under Rows and Columns (both required fields), input the number of rows and columns.

If you are creating a data table, enter a summary for the table under **Summary**. As you now know, summaries are required for data tables as they tell the user the purpose of the table. This information is then made available to screen readers. Summaries do not appear in Edit mode or in Browser Preview mode, but are visible in Screen Reader Preview mode.

Under **Caption**, select **Yes** or **No** to indicate if the table is to have a caption or header or not. Captions are made available to assistive technologies such as screen readers. They are filled in the Edit mode, appear immediately above the table and are center-aligned. Captions are visible in the all view modes.

In data tables, when the **Width** field is left blank, the width of the data table expands as the content is entered into the table.

Under **Cell padding**, enter a number to represent the space you want to appear between the contents of a cell and the cell's border. One (pixel) is the default value.

Under **Cell spacing**, enter a number to represent the space you want to appear between the cells themselves. Two (pixels) is the default value.

Under **Border**, enter a number to represent the thickness of the table gridline. The default border setting for layout tables is invisible or **0.** However, for the author's convenience, a **0** border setting displays a gray border in the Edit mode. One pixel is the default setting for data tables.

Edit Tables Using the Context Menu

Identifying row and column headers is made easy with XStandard, thanks to the pop-up menu seen in the following screenshot.

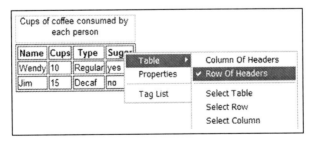

Abbreviations

Using abbreviation tags `<abbr>` can help screen readers to render the expanded version of the abbreviation in order to aid comprehension for the user. The expanded version of the word is placed within the `<title>` attribute as shown in the following screenshot.

```
<abbr title="World Wide Web Consortium">W3C</abbr>
<abbr title="Manufacturer">Mfr.</abbr>
<abbr title="5 5 5 - 1 2 3 4">555-1234</abbr>
```

XStandard makes it easy to use abbreviations and acronyms and will prompt you to enter the **Full Text** for the title attribute.

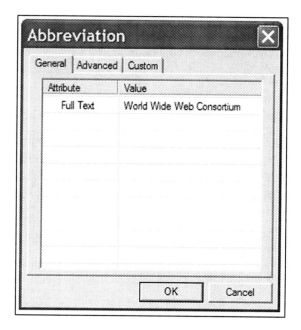

Screen Reader Preview

This is an interesting feature as it lets you see what your site output would be like for a visitor using a screen reader. Screen readers are complicated applications that can be very difficult to learn.

What is Screen Reader Preview?

The Screen Reader Preview shows the author how screen readers will output the content managed through the editor.

The core value of the Screen Reader Preview is in demonstrating how assistive technologies such as screen readers process information in a linear fashion. As I hope you now know, this means that they "read" content from left-to-right, top-to-bottom, regardless of the type of content.

Using the Screen Reader Preview

The Screen Reader Preview is accessed by selecting the Screen Reader Preview button on the toolbar 📷, or by selecting **Toolbar -> Buttons -> Screen Reader Preview**, in the context menu.

To better understand how the Screen Reader Preview works, compare the following screenshots.

The first screenshot shows a collection of mixed content (regular text, formatted text, images and tables) viewed in the Edit mode.

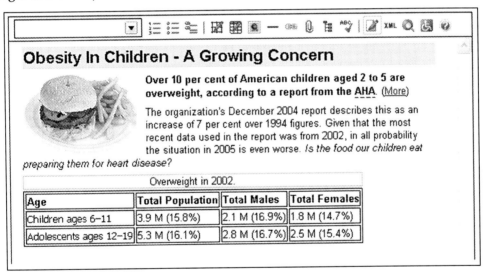

The second screenshot shows the same content viewed in Screen Reader Preview mode. Numbers refer to "Explanatory Notes" that describe accessibility issues raised in the Screen Reader Preview, and include tips for addressing those issues.

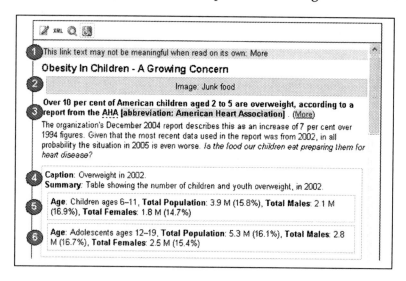

So what does it all mean?

> ● *"This link may not be meaningful when read on its own: More".*

Here, the word **More** is flagged as an unsuitable text for a hyperlink, since **More** would convey no meaning at all, should the users of assistive technologies request to read only the hyperlinks on this page. So make sure your links make sense when read out of the context.

The editor is pre-programmed to warn against using similar expressions as text for hyperlinks.

In this instance, to correct any confusion caused by the hyperlink text **More**, the author can simply return to Edit Mode and replace **More** with more suitable text, such as "Learn more about the AHA" or "Read the American Health Association report".

> ● *"Image: Junk food"*

Here, the image of a burger and fries is replaced by the image's alternate text.

As you now know, alternate text is used by screen readers to describe non-decorative images such as photographs, charts, etc.

The editor ensures that alternate text is available to screen readers by requiring it to be entered for all non-decorative images.

Changes to alternate text can be made in the Edit mode, in the **Image properties** dialog box.

⊙ *"Abbreviation"*

Expanded forms of abbreviations are made available to screen readers.

The expanded form is visible (with a green background) only in the Screen Reader Preview mode. Any changes that you want to make to the expanded form of abbreviations are made in Edit mode, in the **Abbreviation** properties dialog box.

⊙ *"Summary"*

XStandard requires a summary for all data tables, and makes this information available to screen readers.

As you know, summaries are useful to screen readers because they can help situate a table in its proper context. Summaries are only visible in the Screen Reader Preview mode, where the author can review summaries prior to publication.

Summaries can be modified in the Edit mode, in the **Table properties** dialog box.

⊙ *Tables*

Data tables such as the one in our example above typically present content that is understood in relation to column and row headers. As you now know, to make data tables accessible, the presence and content of column and row headers must be flagged to screen readers.

As the Screen Reader Preview confirms, row headers in the table are appropriately flagged by XStandard, in order to make information in the table more accessible.

The only accessibility improvement to the table in question might be to replace the ambiguous letter "M" with the word "million".

Interface Accessibility

XStandard has a fully keyboard-accessible interface which is also great for developers who cannot use a mouse. It also contains many keyboard shortcuts that you may find useful.

The context menu (seen in the previous screenshot) is fully accessible using a keyboard.

When it is available, the context menu is the most accessible means of accessing all features of the editor. The options in the context menu are grouped by type of functionality and differ according to context.

Keyboard Shortcuts

Keyboard shortcuts are useful to everyone, especially users with limited manual dexterity who find it difficult to manipulate pointing devices, such as a mouse. The following keyboard shortcuts can be used inside the editor.

Keyboard shortcuts that can be used in the editor	
Action	WINDOWS
Display context menu	SHIFT + F10
Select all	CTRL + A
Check spelling	F7
Insert line break	SHIFT + ENTER
Undo last action	CTRL + Z
Redo last action	CTRL + Y
Cancel the current task	ESC
Delete selected object	DELETE
Cut	CTRL + X or SHIFT + DELETE
Copy	CTRL + C or CTRL + INSERT
Paste	CTRL + V or SHIFT + INSERT
Page up	PAGE UP
Page down	PAGE DOWN
Apply / remove emphasis to selected text	CTRL + I
Apply / remove strong emphasis to selected text	CTRL + B
Display Hyperlink properties dialog box when text is selected	CTRL + K
Move cursor to the beginning of the next word	CTRL + RIGHT ARROW
Move cursor to the beginning of the current or previous word	CTRL + LEFT ARROW

Move cursor the beginning of the current or previous paragraph or cell	CTRL + UP ARROW
Move cursor to the beginning of the next paragraph or cell	CTRL + DOWN ARROW
Move cursor to the beginning of a line	HOME
Move cursor to the end of a line	END
Move cursor to the top of a document	CTRL + HOME
Move cursor to the end of the document	CTRL + END
Extend selection to the beginning of a line	SHIFT + HOME
Extend selection to the end of a line	SHIFT + END
Extend selection, character-by-character	SHIFT + RIGHT or LEFT ARROW
Extend selection, word-by-word	SHIFT + CTRL + RIGHT or LEFT ARROW
Extend selection, line-by-line	SHIFT + END or HOME + UP or DOWN ARROW
Extend selection, paragraph-by-paragraph	SHIFT + CTRL + UP or DOWN ARROW
Extend selection to the beginning of a document	SHIFT + CTRL + HOME
Extend selection to the end of a document	SHIFT + CTRL + END
Move focus to the next control in the form	TAB
Move focus to the previous control in the form	SHIFT + TAB

For a more detailed look at all of these features, please go to the XStandard website: http://www.xstandard.com, click on the **XStandard Developers Guide** link and look for the **Accessibility** link. There you will find an overview of the new features, how to use them, and what they can do to help you make your websites more accessible.

More Tiny MCE

Tiny MCE has several accessibility enhancements that you saw earlier in this book. It also has the capability of using or adding a plug-in for the "AChecker" accessibility verifier Web service. At time of writing I haven't checked it out, but I have used the A-Prompt checker before and found it useful.

Summary

I really hope that you have enjoyed this brief introduction to accessibility, found it useful, and now feel more confident about using Joomla! to build more accessible websites. For more, keep an eye on the Joomla! forums and don't be shy about posting any queries you have.

If you would like to lean more about accessibility and have some other questions that you would like to ask, I recommend two great online forums where your query will be answered by the planet's best accessibility advocates and developers. They are the WebAIM mailing list (`http://www.webaim.org`) and the Accessify Forum (`http://www.accessifyforum.com/`).

Both are great resources with lots of capable contributors who will always be glad to help.

Index

Section 508, laws 12, 13
UK legislation, laws 11
US legislation, laws 11
lists, accessibility
about 62
adding 63, 64

P

personas, usability
about 21
building 22
using 21

T

tables accessible, accessibility
about 72
associating 79, 80
creating, part 1 73, 74
creating, part 2 74-76
creating, part 3 76-78
guidelines 72
testing 76
trouble 72

U

usability
about 19
definitions 19, 20
user testing 21

V

view modes, XStandard
about 122
browser preview 123
context menu 123, 124
help 123

W

WCAG
about 23
POUR, principles 24
understanding 25
WCAG 1.0, guidelines 23
WCAG 1.0 and 2.0, differences 23

WCAG 2.0, principles 24
Web Content Accessibility Guidelines. *See* **WCAG**

X

XStandard
about 121
correct markup, using 124
data tables 126
decorative versus non decorative images 125
help 123
noise removing, from markup 124
relative values, supporting 125
styles menu 121
tool buttons 122
view modes 122

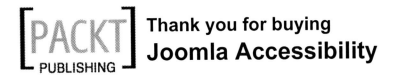

Packt Open Source Project Royalties

When we sell a book written on an Open Source project, we pay a royalty directly to that project. Therefore by purchasing Joomla Accessibility, Packt will have given some of the money received to the Joomla! Project.

In the long term, we see ourselves and you—customers and readers of our books—as part of the Open Source ecosystem, providing sustainable revenue for the projects we publish on. Our aim at Packt is to establish publishing royalties as an essential part of the service and support a business model that sustains Open Source.

If you're working with an Open Source project that you would like us to publish on, and subsequently pay royalties to, please get in touch with us.

Writing for Packt

We welcome all inquiries from people who are interested in authoring. Book proposals should be sent to authors@packtpub.com. If your book idea is still at an early stage and you would like to discuss it first before writing a formal book proposal, contact us; one of our commissioning editors will get in touch with you.

We're not just looking for published authors; if you have strong technical skills but no writing experience, our experienced editors can help you develop a writing career, or simply get some additional reward for your expertise.

About Packt Publishing

Packt, pronounced 'packed', published its first book "Mastering phpMyAdmin for Effective MySQL Management" in April 2004 and subsequently continued to specialize in publishing highly focused books on specific technologies and solutions.

Our books and publications share the experiences of your fellow IT professionals in adapting and customizing today's systems, applications, and frameworks. Our solution-based books give you the knowledge and power to customize the software and technologies you're using to get the job done. Packt books are more specific and less general than the IT books you have seen in the past. Our unique business model allows us to bring you more focused information, giving you more of what you need to know, and less of what you don't.

Packt is a modern, yet unique publishing company, which focuses on producing quality, cutting-edge books for communities of developers, administrators, and newbies alike. For more information, please visit our website: www.PacktPub.com.

Joomla! Template Design

ISBN: 978-1-847191-44-1 Paperback: 250 pages

A complete guide for web designers to all aspects of designing unique website templates for the free Joomla! PHP Content Management System

1. Create Joomla! Templates for your sites

2. Debug, validate, and package your templates

3. Tips for tweaking existing templates

Mastering Joomla! 1.5 Extension and Framework Development

ISBN: 978-1-847192-82-0 Paperback: 380 pages

The Professional Guide to Programming Joomla!

1. In-depth guide to programming Joomla!

2. Design and build secure and robust components, modules and plugins

3. Includes a comprehensive reference to the major areas of the Joomla! framework

Please check **www.PacktPub.com** for information on our titles

Printed in the United States
99544LV00006B/88/A